Hamburgers, Hot Dogs, and Hugs

Real stories of faith, kindness, caring, hope, and humor served up at a small diner with a plate of comfort food and a side of unconditional love.

By

Randy Walters

Foreword by Tara Ijai
Founder of *The Love Glasses Revolution*

Hamburgers, Hot Dogs, and Hugs

Me Youniversity Publishing
ISBN: 978-1-956565-05-8

Printed in the United States of America

Nothing in this book or any affiliations with this book is a substitute for medical or psychological help. If you need assistance, please seek it.

Cover photo by Chanelle Sinclair
Cover designs by Tara Ijai
Back cover photo by John Bratcher

Dedication

To my beloved son-in-law Brice, devoted husband and best friend to my daughter Kelly and amazing daddy to my granddaughter Natalie. Everyone that shared his world knew Brice was a gentle giant of a man, and we are all better humans because of him. Brice passed away unexpectedly due to complications from diabetes while I was writing this book. Please, if you or a loved one has diabetes, stay vigilant in your care. Brice Patrick Hall will forever be loved, remembered, and missed.

Brice Patrick Hall
10/30/1976 - 11/17/2020

The Dude Abides...

We did it!

Thank you for the unyielding support, patience, and hard work of family and friends in bringing this book to fruition.

To my wife Cyndee, who so patiently corrected my drafts, configured the book's photos, and served as the first editor.

To my sister-in-law, Janet Bourbouse, who served as our IT consultant and second editor.

To Geri Koeppel for her expertise as proofreader and final editor.

To my daughters, Kelly and Brynn, for always keeping me grounded, laughing, and on the straight and narrow.

To my dear friends, Tara Ijai, founder of the *Love Glasses Revolution*, who served as both a mentor and wrote the foreword, and Deedra Abboud, for her mentorship and invaluable expertise in spearheading the publishing process.

To all my customers during my ten years in the restaurant business, especially those whose profound impact became the basis for this book.

To my three precious granddaughters:

Cara, 19, who taught me so much about never giving up while I was hospitalized with Covid-19.

Natalie, 14, whose daddy Brice, my son-in-law, passed away unexpectedly after complications from diabetes while writing my book. Natalie showed me how strong one can be after suffering such overwhelming tragedy and how you can still see light even when darkness envelopes you.

Josslyn, 16, younger sister to Cara, who by her Bohemian nature, leads a life of love, kindness, and tolerance with a level of maturity far beyond her 16 years.

Finally, I want to acknowledge the closest group of best friends and poker pals anyone could ever have. They helped and supported my family and me in getting the restaurant started, and for the ten years we were open.

SKOL! That's for you, Tim Borrud.
RIP, my friend.

Back row- Tim, John, Jim, Matt
Front row- Randy, Safet
This was the first poker game after my eye surgery,
with my poker pals showing their support.

Table of Contents

FOREWORD I

PREFACE VII

THE JOURNEY BEGINS 1

PITTSBURGH WILLY'S 9

FOOD FOR THE SOUL 25

WIMPY'S PARADISE 29

WHEN THE SAINTS GO MARCHING IN 33

"I THOUGHT A SAVANT WAS A FRENCH PASTRY" 37

THE THIN MAN IN GRAY 43

THE PERFECT STORM 49

THE BIG TOP COMES TO TOWN 55

THOUGHTS OF SUICIDE 65

WRITER'S BLOCK 73

"WHO WAS THAT ON THE PHONE?" 87

"ARE WEDDINGS ON THE MENU?" 99

"WHERE'S MY MILKSHAKE?" 107

THE MAN IN THE VAN 113

HERE A SIGN, THERE A SIGN, EVERYWHERE A SIGN 121

MUFFINS WITH MUSLIMS 129

TRADING HAM FOR BACON 135

I BEAT THE BEAR 139

ABOUT THE AUTHOR 157

Foreword

I couldn't be more delighted that I get to write the foreword for Randy Walters' book, Hamburgers, Hot Dogs and Hugs!

You see, meeting Randy was a love story from the beginning. Now, please allow me to explain before I go ahead and cause his wife Cyndee to do a double take.

It was February 15th, 2017, and my friend Kristy had reached out to me and told me she saw this restaurant called *Wimpy's Paradise* on the news. She shared with me that he has an inclusive sign outside his restaurant that says, "Free hugs for everyone." We should go get ours! As American Muslims wearing headscarves during a time of rampant hate for the Muslim community, I must tell you; we could really use one!

As my personal mission is all about choosing love, and meeting others in the world who share love, meeting Randy was like meeting a local love celebrity. We rounded up my bestie, Deedra Abboud, who happened to be running for U.S. Senate at the time in Arizona, and she can't refuse a good hot dog.

Yup, three Muslim women walked into *Wimpy's Paradise,* and when we saw Randy, we excitedly told him we were there for the free hugs, and we loved his sign that we had seen on the news! His greeting was beyond warm and welcoming. He had a huge smile and maybe a slight look of fear, but not for any reason you may be thinking. Come to find out, Randy had us in hysterics when we learned that he didn't know what he was going to feed us! Tears of laughter rolled down our faces as he told us that when we first walked in, he was desperately trying to figure out what we could eat on his menu! Imagine his surprise when we ordered what was known as his "cult favorite," Big Willy hot dog and ½ pound hamburgers.

That day we sat at his restaurant for hours. Randy joined us at the table, and we laughed, joked, told stories, and shared a hug. Randy used his restaurant as a source of love and hope for all those that he met. There was not a person that entered his restaurant that was not made to feel special and welcomed. He made everyone feel seen and heard and mostly loved. His love for people was so obvious through the food he served, his sharing of space and service to his community. He was determined to have people leave feeling better than when they arrived.

I am so proud to tell you that we have become great friends. Randy and I have been involved with each other's events and community projects. He is one of my favorite people on the planet and someone I now personally turn to for inspiration when things seem dark.

Randy is a true gift to the world. His flair for storytelling will make you laugh and make you cry. It will give you hope, and it will remind you of all that is good in the world, even if you must go through a little "ugly" to get there.

HAMBURGERS, HOT DOGS, AND HUGS

Read his book and cherish the thought that someone like Randy Walters is out there, making a difference every day. The smallest acts of kindness can make the largest impact. Luckily with Randy's art of storytelling, you get to read all about it. These ripples of love are how we make a better world.

See? I told you! It was such a great love story from the beginning.

Love to all,

Tara Ijai

Bio:

Tara Ijai, a love activist, is a recovering people-pleaser turned love rebel and lives in Phoenix, Arizona, with her husband and two sons. She is the founder of *Love Glasses Revolution*, a movement using stylish heart-shaped glasses to advocate for love starting with self-love. Her goal is to remind herself and others that there is always a choice on how to show up in the world and that love is an action word. You will find her sporting her heart-shaped sunglasses and obsessing over making the world better. Tara's favorite pastime is connecting with people who actively seek to uplift, inspire, and create joy in the world. You can connect with Tara at *hello@myloveglasses.com*.

HAMBURGERS, HOT DOGS, AND HUGS

Preface

Writing this book became a passion for me. It was almost a three-year project, painfully interrupted by the sudden death of a family member, my 20-day hospitalization with COVID-19, and seven months of recovery. The experiences that I am sharing occurred over ten years at my two restaurants. I hope that you will find these stories powerful, inspirational, memorable, and at times humorous. Many will illustrate the strength and resilience of the human spirit, along with interesting anecdotes from a few celebrity customers.

During the process of writing this book and reflecting over my ten years in the service industry, I have come to believe that we all possess the God-given superpowers of love and kindness that can impact someone's day, or possibly, their life.

We seem to have lost our innate sense of kindness and respect toward others. We are more comfortable communicating via keyboard, which seems to have emboldened us to say things that we would never have previously considered saying to someone face to face. Social media has become our communication "kryptonite."

I feel that it's up to all of us to extend a hand to help those in need or hurting by using our superpowers every day,

"USE YOUR SUPERPOWERS OF LOVE AND KINDNESS EVERY DAY"

The Journey Begins

or

How a Dream Became Reality

The journey to "Hamburgers, Hot Dogs and Hugs" began in the small steel mill and coal mining town of Monongahela, about 30 miles south of Pittsburgh, Pennsylvania. It is one of the few small river towns still thriving along the banks of the Monongahela River. I was born in 1953, the second son of Kenneth and Carmel Walters and younger brother to Dennis.

My mom and dad,
Kenneth and Carmel Walters

My brother Dennis and I,
circa 1976

I grew up with parents who, by example, showed love, kindness, and concern for others.

Those were important core values and representative of the small town we lived in. In addition, I had twelve years of a Catholic school education that was guided by nuns who wielded a wooden ruler in their hands but had the student's best interest in their hearts. After graduating in 1971 from Monongahela Valley Catholic High School, I joined the U.S. Navy and served as a hospital corpsman at the Philadelphia Naval Hospital until 1975. A few years earlier, I had reconnected with Cyndee Bourbouse, whom I dated in high school and who was now living in Arizona. I moved to Arizona shortly after being discharged from the Navy and we were married in January of 1976. We later became parents to two beautiful daughters, Kelly and Brynn.

For the next 32 years, my dream to own a restaurant was safely tucked away in the back of my mind. It wasn't until I was fired from my job of 10 years as a painter at a local hospital that I got my sign, my inspiration, or maybe it was a nudge from

God. I was sitting on the couch feeling somewhat depressed, 54 years old, with no college degree, no business or restaurant background, and seriously wondering what my future would hold. It was at that moment I saw a commercial with Dennis Hopper about Ameriprise Insurance. It showed him standing in a field holding a flower in his hand and he says as the beat of the music kicks up, "Some people say dreams are like delicate little flowers. WRONG, dreams are powerful, dreams are what make you say, 'When I'm 64, I want to start a new business.'" I looked at Cyndee and said, "He's talking to me!" And my wife responded, "You've always wanted to own a restaurant like your dad; why not start out by buying a hot dog cart and you'd still be in the food business."

A few days later, I discussed the idea with my friend John Vandemark and he agreed with my wife's idea. I was soon going to be in the hot dog business. Getting my hot dog cart was a huge purchase for me; one I wasn't really prepared to make. I called my good friend Jim Clark and asked him if he wanted to go with me to Phoenix to check out a business that builds hot dog carts. We were welcomed by the owners who explained in detail the joys and concerns that come with a hot dog cart business. Normally, you order your cart and it takes several weeks for them to build it, but we were told that if we wanted one today, they had one available that was just completed. I wasn't ready to commit to the nearly $3,500 needed to buy the cart, but then my friend blurted out, "Let's buy it!"

I had no money or a check with me. I was trying to find an excuse so that I wouldn't make an impulse purchase. Jim said he'd just sold a car for a friend that morning and had $4,000 cash in his pocket. He said I could pay him back when I got my final check and payout from my recent job. Guess what? I bought a hot dog cart!

We hooked it to Jim's truck and brought it home. I worked the cart for three years, creating unique hot dogs and working long hours setting up wherever I could. My family and best bud, John Batcher, pitched in to help at many festivals and gigs. It was hard work and brutal in the Arizona summer months. I was trying to secure a more permanent location for my cart by passing out business cards to several big box stores.

That led to my meeting Brenda Montemorra. She managed Merchant Square, a large antique mall in Chandler, Arizona. After receiving my card, she called and said that they didn't have the need for a hot dog cart, but they were looking for a food vendor to set up indoors and provide food for their customers. My dream of finally having a restaurant, like my dad, was about to come true.

My daughters suggested I use my poker nickname, Pittsburgh Willy, for the hot dog cart, so why not use the same name for the restaurant. Being from the Pittsburgh area, proud of my roots, and with a friendly name like Willy attached, it seemed like the perfect name.

I was about to embark on a new adventure!

My Hometown of Monongahela, PA

*A tugboat traveling on the Monongahela River
as it passes the town of Monongahela*

*A view of Mon City (as the
locals call   it) at night*

*Halloween at Angelo's II in downtown
Monongahela*

HAMBURGERS, HOT DOGS, AND HUGS

Pittsburgh Willy's

or

How a Hot Dog Cart Became a Restaurant

When I opened *Pittsburgh Willy's* doors for the first time in late November 2008, I had three dining tables, each accommodating four customers. For my kitchen, I had a countertop steam table and a hot plate. For the first three months, it was all that I needed. I was literally learning on the job. I had no advertising budget, no restaurant experience, and no business experience, but I had a dream and a vision for the kind of hot dog joint I wanted. Business started out slow, so I had ample time to learn the flow of my "kitchen." Our hours were 11 a.m. to 3 p.m. six days a week. It was a lunch joint, except on Wednesdays when the antique mall remained open until 8 p.m. My time between customers was spent coming up with unique hot dog creations and considering what other menu items I could add with just a hot plate and a steamer. I was using the most expensive quarter-pound all-beef hot dog available. My reasoning was, if I'm going to set myself apart from the already established hot dog places in the area, I needed to serve a better hot dog.

Our original counter on opening day at Pittsburgh Willy's

Word of mouth was spreading. My customer base was growing, and if a customer left without telling me this was the best hot dog they'd ever eaten, I took it personally. I was also excited to introduce Arizonans to some classic Pittsburgh foods, most notably BBQ chipped ham, a Pittsburgh staple. I also needed to come up with an in-house chili recipe for my chili dogs. The canned chili I tried to flavor up wasn't cutting it. Throw in the fact that nobody commented on it was all the motivation I needed to start working on my own chili.

I bought chili-making ingredients and got to work making a small batch every day. I kept exact records of what was in each batch. I would make a small pot every morning. I did this meticulously, till one day almost every customer that ordered a chili dog took the time to tell me it was the best they'd ever tasted. That's when I knew I had my chili recipe dialed in. I knew I was getting close, but on that day, I added one more ingredient that I'm sharing here for the first time. It was Frank's Red Hot Buffalo Wing Sauce. It gave it such a unique and flavorful taste to the chili that my chili dogs became a customer favorite for the next ten years.

With my chili set to go, and my confidence building, I was introduced to the world of restaurant reviews and the angst of waiting for the review to be published. I had no idea that one of my customers a few days back was Jess Harter, who reviewed and profiled restaurants for the East Valley Tribune. On January 29th, 2009, my first review and profile of *Pittsburgh Willy's* was published. I had complete confidence in both the quality of my food and my customer service. However, it wasn't my opinion that was being published for foodies everywhere in the Valley to read. It was a popular food reviewer that was about to share everything he thought about my restaurant. My nervousness soon turned to pure joy when I read the review. He loved *Pittsburgh Willy's*!

With Jess' positive review and detailed profile, I had even more confidence in what I was bringing to the community. I started using Facebook to spread the word about my business. It was completely free and allowed me the opportunity to self-promote my restaurant by posting pictures of my food and sharing anecdotes. It was one of those anecdotes that inspired me to write this book, but it was Jess' review that brought out a local TV station to do a live morning remote from my restaurant. The two TV spots were shown live, one at 8:40 a.m., the other 9:50 a.m., and by 10 a.m., I had 25 people lined up outside waiting to eat, all having watched the TV segments. I had just learned the power of live television!

In the next ten years, I would appear on 42 live morning TV remotes from every major TV network in the valley, along with over 30 in-studio appearances. I was a guest on a live local radio food show several times and eventually had one of my food creations featured on *CNN* and *E! Entertainment*. It was this media exposure that brought a huge brand awareness of my restaurant, both locally and nationally. This resulted in many people seeking out my diner for food, hugs, and comfort. I learned how to create a buzz and put a teaser out on Facebook that oftentimes would generate a media response.

The most incredible example of one of my Facebook posts generating media interest occurred on January 26, 2010. It was the twentieth anniversary of the hottest temperature ever recorded in Phoenix, Arizona: 122 degrees! I posted on Facebook I was offering a regular quarter-pound beef hot dog all day for $1.22. I never sent a tease to any other media sources about the deal.

Imagine my surprise when a news van with a satellite boom pulled up and set up in my parking lot, came into the restaurant, and did a live spot on their noon news about our $1.22 hot dogs! Then as I sat at my counter and watched the news van drive away, another station's van pulled in. Within the hour, every major TV station in Phoenix showed up to do a story on our hot dog deal. Was it a slow news day that day? Probably, but to have every major network out for an unscheduled segment showed both the power of social media and the intense competition between networks. I learned early in business that relationships make a business successful, especially the restaurant business — the relationships with your own family, staff, customers, vendors, and landlords, along with all media formats, including television, print, radio, newspaper, and magazines.

Respect and the public's trust are earned with every meal you serve, every table you touch, and with every customer you encounter. One month after my first review, I received a phone call at the restaurant. The caller said her name was Nikki Buchanan and she was writing a restaurant review for the *Arizona Republic*, the biggest daily newspaper in Arizona. I nervously asked her when she might be coming in. She simply responded, "I've been in a few times and just had some final questions before I finish the review." "Is it a good review?" I sheepishly asked, and she answered in a less than comforting voice, "You'll have to wait to read it!" Having experienced such a positive review just a month earlier didn't ease my nerves. This review would be shared throughout the entire state of Arizona. Once again, while I knew I was building a reputation for great food, service, and an overall fun dining experience, I was still a bundle of nerves. In the restaurant business, the two things you fear most are food critics and the Health Department. A negative review from a food critic or a low score from the Health Department can often make or break a restaurant! As it turned out, she gave me an excellent review, and her only criticism was that on one of her visits, her hot dog bun was cold! It was several weeks later that I contacted her and thanked her for the positive and very detailed review, and to assure her that there would never again be a cold hot dog bun coming out of our kitchen.

Along with Jess' and Nikki's great reviews, there was another unexpected boost for our business, Super Bowl XLIII. My beloved Pittsburgh Steelers would be playing our local NFL team, the *Arizona Cardinals*. I was smack in the middle of Cardinals country with a Pittsburgh named and themed restaurant. My little hot dog place became its own news story in both Pittsburgh and Arizona. The *Pittsburgh Post-Gazette* sent a reporter out to do a story on us, complete with interviews and photographs. The story ended up on their front page, and several smaller local news outlets also reported about our restaurant. That prompted many people living back in the Burgh area to contact friends and relatives that lived out here in Arizona, telling them about the Pittsburgh-themed joint located in Chandler, AZ. The week before and the week after the Super Bowl, I welcomed almost 300 Pittsburgh transplants. My little hot dog joint had just expanded beyond Arizona, and that was just the beginning.

I started receiving phone calls from former Pittsburgh area natives now living in Arizona asking about our pierogies, a huge Pittsburgh favorite. Pierogies, for those who are not familiar with these little "Polish pillows of love," are pockets of pasta stuffed with potatoes and cheese and smothered with butter and onions. YUM! Jess mentioned them in his review, but we weren't sure we could logistically make them a permanent menu item with such a small kitchen and prep area. But, as calls increased about the pierogies, I just started answering, "Yes, we serve them but only on Wednesdays." That was all our small kitchen could handle. They always sold out before closing. We soon bumped up our weekly pierogi numbers to about 300, and we still sold out!

The pierogies were really helping set us apart from all the other hot dog joints in the area. Who knew it would be the pierogies that eventually led to one of the most unusual and critically acclaimed creations we ever served?

One of my regular Wednesday pierogi customers, Eric Ramos, started adding toppings to his regular plate of six pierogies smothered in sweet sauteed onions and butter. The first time he added sauerkraut over the pierogies. The next week he added our in-house no-bean chili over the kraut. His creation wasn't finished nor named yet. On the next visit, he added freshly grated cheddar cheese over the chili. The plate now was heavy, messy, and delicious. His final topping was sliced, grilled kielbasa. And we now had a name for Eric's creation: the *Blitzburgh*. It weighed almost a pound and quickly became one of our most loved dishes and turned Wednesdays into our busiest day. The pierogies also caught the media's attention since not many restaurants in the Phoenix area offered made-from-scratch pierogies.

With my restaurant located inside the antique mall, when *Pittsburgh Willy's* was in the news, the antique mall was, too. The big benefit of all the publicity was that we were also bringing hundreds of new customers to the antique mall. The owner, Mike Moore, and manager Brenda were beyond excited for the boost in customers and the media attention. Mike decided to show his appreciation by transforming his antique stake bed truck into a streetside billboard for *Pittsburgh Willy's*. He positioned it out by the main road where thousands of cars passed by it every day. It soon became a popular photo op for many.

With all the publicity, several Best of Valley awards, great reviews, and a rapidly expanding customer base, we needed more tables and chairs, but there wasn't any available space to expand. Then, management for the antique mall came to me with an idea for some expansion. They would move an area off to the side of our existing three tables, allowing us to add four more. It was about 20 feet of added wall area and fit the four tables nicely.

We, of course, hung all Pittsburgh-related memorabilia on that 20 feet of wall. After just six months in business, we tripled our ability to serve our customers. The only issue was, we already needed more space and tables! By the end of our first year, an opportunity presented itself in the form of a huge room that had its own exclusive entrance. It was rented to a longtime vendor that leased the space for years but wanted to downsize. We had to wait six months till the current occupant officially moved out. We regularly served over a hundred customers a day during that time, with the same kitchen set-up we started with.

It wasn't until May of 2010, 18 months after we opened our doors, that we took possession of the large room. Our remodeling plan was to allow two months to remove some shelving, pull up and create a new floor surface, paint, decorate and open.

We kept the original seven tables in service from 11 a.m. to 3 p.m., then worked late to get the new room ready every evening.

The new dining room(above) and the outdoor patio(below), ready to greet our customers

We were ready to finish up all the details, hoping to open by July, when I suffered a heart attack, making it necessary for us to rethink our plans. My family made the decision to close the restaurant for few days while I recovered, deciding to concentrate on the remodel.

Some of my loyal customers heard about my heart attack, and with the remodel still moving forward, showed up to offer their labor, however it was needed. With the help of my family, friends, and customers, we had our new dining room ready to open on time, July 2010. When we opened our new space, we held a weekend-long celebration.

With the help of some media remotes, lots of social media posts, and the largest staff we ever had, we welcomed hundreds of our regular and first-time customers to both our restaurant and the antique mall.

We now had nine tables in the dining area and a covered patio which included an 8-foot picnic table and three other tables and chairs. We went from a seating capacity of 24 customers to 50. Our kitchen area stayed the same, but we added a double hot plate and an extra tabletop steamer. Every inch of available space was used, allowing only two people to work in the tight kitchen. For the next three years, we continued to put out an unbelievable amount of food, all plated with pride, served with a smile.

While this chapter gives you the background of establishing *Pittsburgh Willy's*, it's the coming chapters that show you the heart and soul of both restaurants and why people sought them out not just for great food, but sometimes for hugs and hope, and comfort.

Food for the Soul

or

How the Hugs Happened

Shortly after I opened my first restaurant in 2008, *Pittsburgh Willy's Gourmet Hot Dogs*, I realized people didn't always come to restaurants just to eat. They often came because they didn't want to be alone and wanted to be alongside others from their community. *Pittsburgh Willy's* was also where I gave my first hug to a customer. It was an elderly gentleman who came in for breakfast every Sunday after church with his wife. They always sat at the same table, clasped hands over their food while praying, then after dining, walked into the attached antique mall to, as he told me, "Walk off the delicious calories we just enjoyed."

I hadn't seen this sweet couple for several weeks, and then one day, the elderly gentleman walked in alone and sat at their regular table. He ordered his usual and dined quietly as I watched him from across the room. After a while, I went to his table and asked him, "Where's your bride?" He looked up at me, thanked me for asking, and softly said she had passed away two weeks ago. I knew the answer before he shared it with me, but it hit me hard all the same. I offered my condolences and asked if there was anything I could do for him.

As he stood up, he said, "Just keep this table for US every Sunday." I opened my arms to offer him a hug, and he opened his arms to me. We hugged, a long, tight, much-needed hug, and as we stepped back, he looked at me and said, "Thank you, see you next Sunday." The gentleman returned every Sunday for almost a year, always sitting at the same table, ordering the same breakfast, and only leaving after we hugged.

I never knew when the next hug would be our last hug, but eventually, he stopped coming in. I kept his table open for several weeks, but I never saw him again. I never knew his name, but it didn't matter. We both knew our feelings, and I took comfort in knowing that he and his wife, at least for a while, allowed my little restaurant to become a regular part of their Sunday routine. I will never forget what he told me after one of our hugs. He said, "You know that I could eat breakfast anywhere, but this has become OUR place, and this is OUR table, and I look forward to OUR hugs."

That comment made me realize how powerful and important a hug can be, and I committed at that moment to offer hugs to anyone that wanted or needed one. That commitment resulted in sharing over 5,000 hugs before I retired, ten years after I opened my first restaurant.

*Proud to receive the "Best Hugger in the
Valley" award from
the "Best of 2017" issue of Phoenix
Magazine*

Wimpy's Paradise

or
How Two Became One

I wanted to incorporate the quality of food and customer service that was my dad's trademark when he opened his restaurant in 1939. I remember as a teenager having a heart-to-heart talk with my dad. After he shared some lessons about life with me, he asked if I had any questions.

First, I asked, "Why did you close your restaurant, and my second question was, if I was ever to have a restaurant like you had, what would I need to do to be successful?" His first answer was that his lease was up, and he and my mom decided to have another child — me. Since the uncertainty of the restaurant business and long hours didn't seem best suited to raise a family, he went to work for Prudential Insurance Company. That provided him with a stable income and security. But it was the answer to my second question that was forever seared in my heart and brain. He said there are two things you need to do to have a successful restaurant. "Always use the best quality and freshest ingredients available, and make sure every customer knows that *THEY* are the most important customer."

Those words became my business mantra and no doubt resulted in many customer interactions that went beyond simply serving food in a diner and became a place where customers sought out so much more. My last question was, "Do you have any regrets in life?" He answered softly, "Only that I closed and never reopened *Wimpy's Paradise*."

My dad with three of his regulars at the original Wimpy's Paradise circa 1940

Opening day at the original Wimpy's Paradise in 1939

During my years at *Pittsburgh Willy's*, I learned the value of serving kindness and love with every order of food delivered. I closed *Pittsburgh Willy's* in January of 2013, intending to move it a few miles south to historic downtown Chandler, and open *Wimpy's Paradise* around the corner. But a second heart attack changed those ambitions, and I combined both concepts into one location. *Wimpy's Paradise* and my dad's dream were reborn on February 14, 2013, 74 years after the original opened! I was now ready to continue my dad's dream and bring back *Wimpy's Paradise*.

I combined menu items from both restaurants. This allowed my faithful customers who enjoyed my *Pittsburgh Willy's* menu to still enjoy their favorite foods, but now they also had a chance to enjoy Hamburgers, Hot Dogs, and Hugs.

Mexican Hot Tamales in Monongahela in 1939?
I guess I know where I got my quirky food
creations and promotions from.
Thanks Dad!

When the Saints Go Marching In

or

How to Save a Quarter

Every year in November, the San Marcos Resort hosts a classic jazz festival just up the street from my restaurant. Jazz artists from seasoned pros to up-and-coming youngsters bring three days of jazz to town. It's a party atmosphere that has jazz musicians playing on the sidewalks of downtown Chandler and even some spontaneous a cappella pop-ups. But the crown jewel of the jazz event is the annual Thursday evening "all-hands-on-deck" Dixieland band parade.

Musicians, dancers, and singers strut past the businesses and restaurants while playing and singing, "When the Saints Go Marching In," and about 100 colorfully dressed, boa-wearing old-time jazz folk strut their stuff, twirl colorful umbrellas, and get the party officially started.

My restaurant had become a regular eating place for many of the festival attendees. I loved sitting and talking with them, hearing their stories and passion for jazz, many performing well into their nineties.

Two very sweet, jazz-loving ladies in their golden years allowed me to experience one of the most delightful encounters with customers that I ever had. They both ordered a small hamburger with a side of potato salad. We served our burgers open-faced, lettuce, tomatoes, and pickles on the side under the top bun. This allowed each customer the choice of how to dress their burger. I checked on the lovely ladies a few times while they enjoyed their lunch. When they finished eating, they walked up to pay at the counter.

The one lady had her plate with her. She set the plate on the counter in front of me and I saw the lettuce, tomato, and pickles just as they were when I delivered their food. Her check total was $6.75. She rooted through her change purse and as she was searching for her money, she looked at me said, "Sir, I didn't eat the lettuce, tomato, and pickles, so can I get an adjustment?" I had never been asked to discount a ticket for any food we delivered that may have gone unused, but my somewhat shocked expression quickly turned to thoughts of how beautiful this moment was. I said, "Of course, I will gladly take a quarter off." She smiled and thanked me.

For the price of a quarter, I made this sweet customer's day. I never saw her again after that magical moment. I only hope she's still getting adjustments for whatever she leaves on her plate!

HAMBURGERS, HOT DOGS, AND HUGS

"I Thought a Savant was a French Pastry"

or

How I Met the World's Only Acquired Musical Savant

"I really shouldn't have one, but I see you sell chocolate malt shakes." Those were the first words Derek spoke to me. I'll never forget the slight smile and his sparkling, expressive eyes. He sported a tight black T-shirt that drew you to his muscular tattooed arms. Each arm had a music staff of notes, spiraling gently from each wrist and disappearing under his sleeves. I knew instantly the man in front of me had an amazing story... and boy does he!

He's one of only 50 acquired savants in the world, which means that a brain trauma results in acquiring an instant and amazing ability for mathematics, calendar calculations, art, or mechanical or spatial skills. But Derek is the only known acquired savant in the world to become a musical virtuoso! He suffered his trauma on October 27, 2006, at age 39. He dove headfirst into the shallow end of a swimming pool trying to catch a football. His head hit the bottom of the pool and he was taken to the hospital with a severe concussion and some memory and hearing loss. A few days after the accident, he was released from the hospital and visited his friend who was with him at the time of the accident. His friend was a musician and had an old electric keyboard setup.

Derek felt drawn to the keyboard. He stood up, walked to it, and sat down. He had never played a keyboard before, but he laid his hands on the keys and began to play for almost five hours! Beautiful music flowed from the keyboard, and he described his mental vision this way. As he closes his eyes, he sees black and white geometric squares moving from left to right. It's not repetitive music going in a circle, but one continuous song. Although he could neither compose nor play, he would discover that he could recall and play a piece of music as if it had been etched in his mind's eye. Derek has since released an album, traveled the world sharing his most unique story, and advocates for and actively helps those who are homeless — something he was passionate about before his brain injury.

As Derek enjoyed his chocolate malt, we sat and chatted. He told me he was in town doing a motivational presentation with Montel Williams and that he'd walked by my restaurant a few times. He was drawn to the old-fashioned malt sign. This time as he passed, he decided to stop in and indulge his weakness for a chocolate malt.

*So **that's** a Twilly dog!*

He also took a special interest in one of my unique hot dog creations called the *Twilly* dog. It's a beef hot dog nestled inside a sliced Twinkie for the bun, then topped with peanut butter and peppered bacon. He seemed very interested in the *Twilly* and said he'd be back in before he left town to try one of those.

True to his word, he came back that evening with some friends and they hesitantly tried one of the most unusual hot dogs I'd ever created. The verdict was that they loved it! We chatted again for a few hours, keeping my restaurant open late and simply enjoying what was already becoming a real friendship. As Derek left, he asked if I'd be at the restaurant early the next morning. He wanted to gift me a signed copy of his book, "My Beautiful Disaster," before he left for the airport. I told him I'd be in early prepping for the day. We hugged, and he and his friends left.

Saturday morning, I was back in the kitchen, music blaring and the front door locked as I prepped for the day. I wasn't sure exactly when Derek would be stopping by, so every five minutes or so I'd back up from my cutting table to look out towards the front to see if Derek was standing there. I was slicing, dicing, and rocking to the music when something in my brain said, "Step back, he's here!" I backed up, looked toward the front, and there was

Derek just standing there. I quickly opened the door and told him, "I felt like a voice was telling me you were here and that's what made me look." Derek just smiled and said quietly, "Well, I was kind of thinking, hey Randy, I'm out here and the door is locked." He then momentarily stunned me by saying, "I've experienced that before." He was in a hurry, so I couldn't pursue that comment further, as badly as I wanted to. After we hugged, he handed me his signed book and a leather wristband that he wanted me to have. We shook hands, and as he left,

I felt like I had just experienced a magical moment with a magical human who selflessly now shares his miraculous life with all of us.

Meeting Derek Amato for the first time at Wimpy's

Oh, and before the brain injury, when Derek thought a savant was a French pastry, I thought magic was just fantasy. Now Derek is a savant, and I believe in magic!

Note: While writing Derek's chapter, I received an e-mail that he had been in a horrific head-on automobile accident. I suspended writing this chapter till I was certain Derek was going to recover. He suffered many severe injuries, and his road back has been long, painful, and difficult. But in typical Derek fashion, he moved on with determination and is back to speaking, writing, and playing the piano. He still suffers from severe migraines that have plagued him since his diving accident, but now also lives with residual aches and pains from his car accident. Most of Derek's interviews, videos, and his Ted Talk can be found on YouTube. You can also purchase his book, "My Beautiful Disaster," on Amazon.

The Thin Man in Gray

or

How I Got a Second Chance to Serve an Angel

It's not often in life that we get a second chance to do the right thing, but I got such a chance in late June of 2016. It was already close to 100 degrees out, and my only focus was to finish filling my gas tank, drive the three miles to my restaurant, and enjoy the air conditioning. As I pulled up to the stoplight, I was the lead car in the left turn lane. While waiting for my green arrow, I noticed a very thin man crossing in the far crosswalk. He was wearing long gray sweatpants and a matching gray hoodie pulled up over his head. He carried a small backpack that most likely carried all his earthly possessions. I just stared at him crossing the street, wondering how hot he must be. Then something spoke to me. It was telling me to check on this man. As I made a left turn, a city bus was just pulling into place at the bus shelter, blocking me from making a safe right turn into the convenience store. I continued to drive and looked in the rearview mirror, where I saw the man in gray leaning against the bus shelter as the bus pulled away. Yes, I felt a twinge of regret for not trying harder to pull in and check on the man but rationalized that he would be okay, and I needed to get to work and cool off.

We opened for business at 11 a.m., and we had a very busy lunch that day. It was now about 2:30 p.m., the time between lunch and dinner when we were always the slowest. As I was sitting on my tall stool behind the cash register, I thought about the thin man in gray. I wondered if he was okay, if he finally got a bus or someone gifted him something to eat and drink. My restaurant was three miles from where I saw him, and by now the temperature outside was 106. I couldn't seem to shake the nagging guilt of not stopping to see if he was okay. I suddenly lifted my eyes to the front of the store, and there he was, the thin man in gray. He had a hand cupped to each side of his face pressing against the window, straining to see inside! There were 30 other restaurants around me in the downtown Chandler area, but here he was, looking into my restaurant. Three miles and five and a half hours from the time I saw him at the bus stop. I jumped up quickly and walked to the front of the restaurant. I opened the door, stood in the doorway, and asked him if he was hungry. He answered in a very soft voice, "Yes, but I have no money."

I said, "It's okay. Just take a seat at one of the patio tables behind you, and I'll bring you some food." It was then I noticed his hands and fingernails were caked with grime, his straggly beard and thin face were dirty. His sneakers had toes sticking out where the fabric had worn, but his eyes, his eyes sparkled! I served him two quarter-pound hot dogs, potato salad, and two sodas. He softly said, "Thank you." I walked back inside the restaurant, stood back a distance from the window, and watched him eat. He devoured the food and never once looked up from the plate. I went back outside and asked if he would like some more food. He quietly answered, "No, thank you." I said that I would be right back and hurried inside to grab him two more cold waters to take with him. It took ten seconds at the most, but when I returned, the thin man in gray was gone!

My restaurant was located midway on a covered breezeway, with about five stores next to me in either direction, about 100 yards from the main street. It wouldn't be possible for ANYONE to be out of my line of sight that quickly. He would have had to stand up, reach over for his backpack and run faster than humanly possible for me not to see him. There was a barber from next door, Scottie, who was outside smoking a cigarette when the man first sat down. Scottie was still there when I returned with the bottles of water. I asked Scottie if he saw the man walk away and he said, "You mean the homeless-looking guy at your table?" "Yes," I said, "Did you see him get up and leave?" Scottie said, "Now that you mention it, No!"

There was a moment of questioning, did this really happen? But those thoughts were fleeting as I had these intense feelings that God was the one who spoke to me that morning while sitting at that stoplight. That it was God that sent an angel to test me, and thankfully, gave me a second chance to do the right thing. Every morning I drove about eight miles, making three stops for fresh produce, meat, and supplies.

For three years, I'd often pass the same homeless souls walking or laying on a bench with their possessions next to them. I had NEVER seen the thin man in gray before, and I've never seen him since. There's no doubt in my mind or in my heart that I earlier failed to, and later was given a second chance to do the right thing……. and serve an angel.

HAMBURGERS, HOT DOGS, AND HUGS

The Perfect Storm

or

How Three Strangers Found Comfort and Support in a Diner

It was February 15, 2018, mid-afternoon, and the restaurant was empty. I was sitting alone, listening to some Beatles music on the record player. The front door opened and one of my regular customers, Thalia, walked in. She took a few steps, stopped, and just looked at me. She continued toward me, crying softly as I opened my arms to hug her. I held her and asked her what was wrong? She looked up at me and said she'd been sad all day after dropping her son off at school. She said she just needed to be here, feel safe, express her fear, and find comfort. She slid into a booth, and after I got her a cold drink, I sat across from her. She told me how for the first time she felt angst and the real fear that anytime she dropped her son off at school, it could be the last time she would see him.

It was the day after the Marjory Stoneman Douglas High School shootings in Parkland, Florida. We talked about that tragedy and the impact all school shootings were having on students, staff, and families. Students today were training for scenarios that we never heard of or could even imagine. It was a difficult and emotional conversation.

After several minutes, the front door again opened. Barb, another friend and customer, stood in the doorway. As she approached us, I stood up, greeted her with a hug, and she joined Thalia in the booth. She said, "Today would have been my son Michael's twenty-eighth birthday. His birthdays are always hard." Her son Michael was killed by a red-light runner fourteen years earlier at age 14. "I was driving up Arizona Ave and feeling sad, thinking about Michael, and I just had to come here. This was where I needed to be right now." Barb shared the heartbreaking story of Michael's death. She told us that her son will forever be 14 and how her son's tragedy inspired her to become a high visibility activist for a coalition called Red Means Stop Traffic Safety Alliance. It was created to bring awareness of how devastating and life-changing running a red light can be and hopefully prevent another family from experiencing the lifelong grief that her family is living. Barb has gained national recognition for her work. As the three of us sat, listened, and comforted each other, I felt a deep sense of purpose in that my restaurant had again become more than just a diner serving food!

But the story doesn't end here. While the three of us were wiping tears from our cheeks, the front door again opened and in walked a young girl. She was crying and visibly upset. I immediately recognized her. It was a young Muslim girl who had been to my restaurant many times with her mother. She was just 15 years old and always wore traditional Muslim dress. She isn't required to but is proud of who she is and her beliefs.

I'd learned from earlier visits that she's been a frequent target of harassment, and it was exactly that which brought her to *Wimpy's Paradise* that day. We all three stood to welcome and hug her. She then sat next to me in the booth. We had cold drinks and sat together for the next hour just talking, listening, sometimes laughing, and often crying, but we were there for each other.

It seems she was in the downtown area with her mom. They had separated for a while when she was approached by an older gentleman who began to assault her verbally. She just quietly turned to walk away, but the man's tirade continued. Instead of looking for her mom, she walked the few doors down to *Wimpy's*, where she knew she would be safe and, more importantly, accepted!

As the three customers all stood to leave, I walked them to the door. We exchanged heartfelt hugs, and after they left, I put on another Beatles record and sat alone in the booth, just allowing myself to process what had happened. I always prided myself and encouraged my staff to create an environment in our restaurants that provided not only amazing food, but a place where everyone felt welcomed, accepted, safe, and loved. I'd say that day was the validation that we accomplished our goal.

Barbara's son, Michael's "Forever 14"
birthday photo
February 15, 1990 - August 28, 2004
RIP

***For more information on the Red Means Stop Traffic Safety Alliance, go to the website: *redmeansstop.org*. They also have a Facebook page titled Red Means Stop Traffic Safety Alliance.**

HAMBURGERS, HOT DOGS, AND HUGS

The Big Top Comes to Town

or

How I Took an Order from a 2 x 4

Every year for the past ten years, the *Zoppé Family Circus* came to town. They always set their big top, one-ring circus near downtown Chandler. It's always during Christmas week through New Year's, and it's become a great holiday tradition for many families. The *Zoppé Family Circus* started in Europe in 1842. It was literally born out of love. Napoline Zoppé, a street performer, wandered into Budapest, Hungary looking for work, and it was there he met a beautiful equestrian ballerina named Ermenegilda, and she captured Napoline's heart.

However, Ermenegilda's father disapproved of the relationship, as he felt a street clown was beneath his daughter. But filled with love, hope and dreams, the young couple ran away to Venice, Italy, and founded the *Zoppé Family Circus*, which still bears the family's name. Nearly 100 years later,

Napoline's great-grandson, Alberto, inherited the circus. Today, the *Zoppé Family Circus* continues with Alberto and Sandra's children, Giovanni, Tosca, and Carla, along with their spouses. Giovanni is now the driving force and director behind the circus.

While writing this chapter, Giovanni's sister, Tosca, and their mother Sandra, were both seriously injured in a head-on collision while returning to Arkansas after their Arizona shows, their last stop every circus season. Tosca has been unable to perform the past year and is still rehabbing from her injuries. Matriarch Sandra passed after several months to join the love of her life Alberto, who died in 2009. Sandra's last words to her beloved husband speak to his lifelong passion and proud Italian heritage, "You know, Alberto, you're going to be so happy because you're going to be in heaven. Jesus will be there waiting with his arms open and standing right by him will be your mother. She'll be waiting with a big plate of spaghetti." It was a devastating loss for her family and the circus family that so loved and revered her.

My restaurant was just a quarter of a mile south of where the circus was set up every year. I had attended a performance once with all my granddaughters, but never had the pleasure of meeting any of the performers or crew. Then one day, a most pleasant gentleman walked into my restaurant and ordered some food.

As I tried to do with all my customers, I sat with him and thanked him for dining with us. He introduced himself as Joey and said that he worked for the circus that was in town. He was so soft-spoken and just smiled all the time. He shared with me his journey of leaving a regular job and joining a traveling circus. I was mesmerized by his story because isn't that every child's dream at some time, especially after attending a circus? I told Joey it had been several years since I attended their circus and that I'd love to feed the entire circus crew in exchange for circus tickets. Joey said he would have to check with Giovanni, but it sounded like a great idea. Joey left and stopped back the next day. He said Giovanni told him, "Let's do it," so I gave Joey a paper menu and told him to take it with him, write down everybody's order, and then bring it back. Also, to let me know what time works best for everyone. Joey returned about an hour later, holding a two-foot piece of 2x4 wood in his hand, and on it everyone's order written next to their names. It perfectly exemplified the circus mantra, *make it work with what you got!*

When the circus folks arrived, it was pure excitement. There were acrobats, tumblers, highwire artists, and many other circus  performers from all around the globe — all so friendly and appreciative to be enjoying a meal away from their traveling trailers. They shared stories of their childhood, their homelands, and what life was like as a traveling circus performer. They were humble, kind, and just all so happy!

The next night, I took my entire family, nine of us, to see the circus. Giovanni greeted us himself, and the performers that we fed all graciously approached me and once again thanked me for their meals. In a small family circus, everyone has several jobs. The young man selling us drinks and popcorn was later swinging from a high perch, doing death-defying flips and twists. The furthest seats are only about 20 feet from the action, so you do feel an intimacy with each performer. For that evening, we all felt like a part of the circus family.

It's a Zoppé family tradition to lower the big top on the evening of the last performance, and it's an all-hands-on-deck event. With the big top lowered and before it's removed, all the crew gathers for a closing night celebration of food, drink, and fun. With Giovanni's blessing, I provided the food for the breakdown for the next two years. At sundown, with the dim glow of lights and the scurrying of workers lowering the big top, my two youngest granddaughters and I arrived to feed the hungry crew. We got to meet almost everyone and hear lots of great circus stories. In a display of classic circus hospitality, Jay Walther, Tosca's husband and the ringmaster, took all three of us to the stables to see the beautiful horses that we watched so regally perform during the show. He was so informative and never rushed my granddaughters. He just answered all their many questions as they petted the horses. The best moment that night was meeting the family matriarch, Sandra! Her eyes sparkled, and you could tell everyone revered her. She was a gentle, sweet soul who was obviously mother to everyone in the crew, not just her own children.

2019 was the last year that the *Zoppé Family Circus* was scheduled and performing. Like all live circus shows, the pandemic forced them to cancel nationwide. It meant financial ruin for many of the already dwindling circuses, and many big tops would never be raised again, but Giovanni couldn't accept his beloved circus ending this way.

For over 170 years, his family kept the *Zoppé Family Circus* alive during wars and many other catastrophic world events. In the circus world, the show must go on, but how?

Giovanni and his crew took a huge gamble and created a unique venue: an interactive circus.

They brought together circus goers and performers in America's only COVID-19-safe, well-mitigated outdoor environment.

The Zoppé multimedia drive-in circus was born!

Giovanni as Nino promoting the new interactive circus with the community

The multi-media circus

It was the only continuous performing circus in America in 2020. Circus goers sat in their cars in a half-moon formation of several rows facing a stage where the circus acts performed. They tuned into the sounds of the circus through a live radio feed, and instead of clapping their approval for the artists' performances, they blew their car horns!

Along with other performers, Giovanni walked around each town where they performed dressed in their showtime outfits promoting their new circus format by waving, juggling, and tumbling. They were sharing with a pandemic-weary world that you can still enjoy a safe, fun, family night out and that the circus had come to town!

Giovanni Zoppé and I
standing outside the
Big Top

**For performance dates and more information about the Zoppé Italian Family Circus, go to *www.zoppe.net*

HAMBURGERS, HOT DOGS, AND HUGS

Thoughts of Suicide

or

How a Hug Could Change a Life

Can a hug save a life, or two lives? Maybe! I got to the restaurant early that morning. It was one of Arizona's rare cloudy days with a good chance of rain. On days like this, I always did my shopping early and got to the restaurant to brew up some coffee, play some records from the '60s and '70s and relax before starting the day's prep work. I also always put out an A-frame sign on the breezeway so anyone walking by knows that even before we open for business, they can still come in for a free hug or a cup of coffee. My sign that morning simply said, "Arizona's best hot dogs and hamburgers served here along with the world's best hugs. No purchase necessary for a hug." I often had people stopping in just for a hug. Sometimes they would share why the hug was important or needed at that time, and often it was just a hug, a thank you, and they were out the door.

Little did I know that I was about to experience one of the most emotional and powerful hugs that I would ever give. It was just after 9 a.m., two hours before I opened. I was sitting at a table, sipping coffee, and reading the morning paper when I heard the door open. I looked up and saw a young woman, maybe in her mid-twenties, standing in the doorway holding the door open. She asked in a very soft and shaky voice, "Are you the hugger?" "Yes," I replied, and she let go of the door quickly. As she rushed toward me, she pushed her long blonde hair over her shoulder, and with her lips trembling, tears fell from her eyes. As I stood up, she literally fell into my arms. She was sobbing uncontrollably, and she wrapped her arms tightly around me. My arms embraced her, and as she sobbed into my chest, we hugged tightly. No words were spoken.

As with all hugs, I always wait for the person initiating the hug to let go because I have no idea what the person's reasons or needs are at that moment. After what seemed like several minutes, she relaxed the hug and slowly pulled away while looking up at me with watery eyes and black lines of mascara dripping down her cheeks. It was at that very moment that we both understood the incredible power of the hug. I reached out and gently placed my hands on each of her shoulders and asked what I could do for her. "Would you like to sit and talk, or can I call someone for you?" She swallowed hard and said, with just a hint of a smile, "No, thank you, sir. I'm OK now." As she stepped back, she turned slowly, walking towards the front door. I stood silently, not knowing what to say, and then she stopped, turned around, and said, "I'm really OK now, sir, thank you so much for the hug."

She then looked down at the floor for a moment, as if she was deciding whether to share more or turn and walk out. I continued to simply look at her, still uncertain as to what to say when she looked up, smiled again, and spoke with a deliberate firmness in her voice. "Sir, I need to tell you something. I walk down the street, across from here, every day. I've never been on this side of the street, ever, and as I walked parallel to your restaurant, something told me to come to this side of the street. I listened, as I had nothing to lose when I saw your sign offering free hugs. I knew then why I crossed the street."

I said to her, "Thank you for listening to your thoughts. I'm so happy you walked over here. I think we both needed that hug." She then said, "Sir, you don't understand. I was walking home from work to kill myself." I struggled to speak, not knowing if there were any words that could help or comfort her. She then smiled, wiped the tears from her cheeks, and lifted her head up. She looked at peace and said, "I promise I'll come back whenever I need a hug." Then she turned and walked out the door. I stood in place, processing what had just happened. I had feelings of warmth, comfort, and awe, knowing God spoke to her and empowered her to cross the street for her first time and literally showed her a sign! I believe that God also made sure it was one of those rare cloudy days in Arizona that brought me to work early. She never came back for a hug, and I don't know what happened to her, but I do know that on that morning, she walked away knowing she was sent to and found a place where without judgment, she could just feel love, hope, and the power of a hug.

It was nearly one year later when a gentleman who looked to be in his mid- to late fifties walked into the restaurant. We had just opened five minutes earlier, and he was my first customer. He said he recognized me as the owner and the guy who gives hugs from an article in the newspaper that morning. My picture was on the front of the story, and it just happened I was wearing the same shirt and fedora as in the picture. We hugged. It was a firm hug, maybe a few seconds and then he relaxed and backed away from me. Without making eye contact, he asked for a hamburger and a milkshake. He took a seat at the table directly in front of the register. As his food and shake were being prepared, I discreetly kept an eye on him. He was very fidgety, fingers strumming on the table. At times, he would lift both hands to cover his face and take in deep breaths. I served him his order, and he thanked me again without making eye contact. As he took a bite out of his burger, several customers arrived.

I now had a line of customers in front of me waiting to place their orders. The man sitting at the table apologetically interrupted and asked if I could bring him a to-go box and a pen and paper. I delivered him the items he requested, but the only thing close by to write on was one of my guest checks. He thanked me and packed up his burger. As I took my customer's order, I noticed him writing, and then place the guest check face down, and he rested the pen on top of it. He stood up and I excused myself and rushed out to the walkway. I looked in both directions, but I never saw him. I walked back inside and stopped to pick up the pen and his note. I set it aside to read after I was finished taking orders.

It read, "I really just came for the hug. One day at a time, just trying to find reasons to live. Thanks for the hug." He signed it with only a first name.

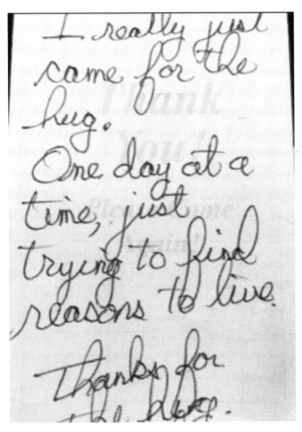

Like the young lady above, I never saw this gentleman again, and I have at times struggled wondering what may have happened to either of them.

But, again, I take comfort in knowing that during his time at my restaurant, he felt both kindness and the warmth of a caring hug and, just maybe, a reason to keep living.

*** If you are experiencing depression with thoughts of suicide, please call the National Suicide Prevention Lifeline 24/7 at 1-800-273-8255.

Writer's Block

or
How Jesus Took the Wheel!

Before reading the chapter below, it requires the following explanation. I was sitting on the second-floor patio of Puro, a cigar bar located in downtown Chandler. I spent many days sitting at the same table, enjoying a cigar and a bourbon while writing. But this was unlike any other day. I'd been uncertain as to how to begin this chapter. It involved a very spiritual moment that was the focus of the entire chapter. I always arrived at *Puro* at 10 a.m. when they opened. This day I got there well after 3 p.m. I ordered my bourbon and lit my cigar. When I went to open my red case that I always brought with

The day and place where Jesus took the wheel. Use your imagination and you can see the red pen and writing!

73

me, instead of the many notebooks I usually had, there were only two, and my three black pens and one green pen were missing. Just my two red correction pens were in my bag. So, I wrote in ONLY red ink. The significance of writing the entire chapter in RED ink was brought to my attention by my friend Gina, and only after I posted on Facebook that an amazing experience had just occurred!

I also mentioned on the post that for the first time, in all my writings for the book, I started writing and didn't stop until I completed the chapter, in about 15 minutes. Gina texted me, and said "Do you know what just happened?" "No," I replied. Gina responded, "God wrote this chapter FOR you." She continued to tell me in a very excited voice, "In the Bible, all God's words are in RED ink." This would help explain why this chapter is so special and why I believe that God wrote this chapter through me. The words all came to me quickly and nonstop. And with my arthritic fingers,

I kept up the best I could with fast-flowing words. That's why every word and punctuation in this chapter has not been changed; I chose to leave it as it was penned and would never alter any sentence structure or punctuation. While it was divinely spoken to me, it was just a man with arthritic fingers and just a red pen putting His words to paper.

An Unexpected Ministry

I consider myself spiritual, not religious, in that I don't worship in a shared community that involves a relationship with God. I grew up and was raised Catholic. I attended 12 years of Catholic school. Those 12 years had nothing to do with my eventually distancing myself from the Catholic Church. It was a gradual descent from standing as a "good" Catholic to my acceptance with a personal relationship with God. I spent many years as a Christmas and Easter Catholic, but I also made sure my daughters received their early sacraments.

Eventually I stopped attending church. Do I miss the support and community of being part of an organized religion? In hindsight, I would say yes. Which played a big, no, a huge role in opening my first restaurant, *Pittsburgh Willy's*. Unbeknownst to me, my restaurant became my ministry, my customers became my community, and my restaurant a place of acceptance and support for everyone that walked through the doors. It wasn't planned that way, it evolved that way. Into a place where people could find comfort, solace, and darn good food. Not only to feed their tummies, but also a place to nourish their souls.

I had been open just over a year learning as I go. I had no prior business experience and absolutely no restaurant experience. I felt strongly that I could open a simple hotdog joint, just like my dad did in 1938. As a young child my dad served as a combat engineer, stationed in France during

World War Two. Upon learning that my dad owned a restaurant, he was recruited to mess cook. My favorite story that he shared with me was classic. My dad came across a French girl whose family owned a farm. They raised several farm animals and had a lot of chickens, and that meant lots of eggs. My dad did some negotiating and was able to get 15 dozen eggs. He snuck them back to his tent but not before he made breakfast for the girl's family. Once he was safely in his tent, he cracked open all the eggs and carefully placed all the broken half shells in a box. He secured a large trash barrel, and he filled the barrel with debris up to about four inches from the top. He then piled the broken shells on top of the debris. To everyone it looked like a trash drum full of eggshells. Every Monday my dad pretended dump the shells, but he put the barrel in his tent, unnoticed by the soldiers who rushed through breakfast. Fresh eggs were rare anywhere in France in World War Two, and the army only supplied powdered eggs. Now I can only assume that every detail of the story is true. Dad said he set the trash drum near the mess line entrance, where the soldiers could see them while they passed through the line. They all thought they were all getting fresh eggs and always thanked my dad for having fresh scrambled eggs for them. My dad was either a very resourceful cook, especially in wartime, or a gifted storyteller. I believe that he was very resourceful.

I mentioned earlier how my restaurant became my Ministry. I never called it that. That awareness came from a gentleman named Mark Smith, that I was about to meet at my hot dog joint. Mark owned a several BBQ places around the valley, and accompanied his wife to the Antique mall, to check out my place. Seems some of his customers had tried our BBQ pulled pork sandwich and really liked it. They told Mark about our little joint and our good food, so he came with his wife to check us out while she shopped. As I was closing, Mark approached me and introduced himself. He said he had been observing me with my customers for a while, and as we shook hands, he looked me in the eyes and said, "Do you know what you have here?" "A hot dog joint" I replied. "Not just that but I've been watching you interact with your customers, serving them food and touching every customer and sitting with them, listening to them. This is your ministry." I never forgot those four words, and I recognized why he said it. That was the moment that God let me know I was exactly where I was meant to be.

Moments and Memories

"Who Was That on the Phone?"

or

How We Rubbed Elbows with Hollywood!

"Who was that on the phone?" my wife asked. I responded very matter of fact, Billy Gardell from Mike & Molly, and he's on his way here for lunch! She gave me that "come on, who was it really" look, and I smiled and said, "Really, Billy is driving here now." Having a restaurant does often afford you the opportunity to meet some famous people. I've had several celebrities visit my restaurants, but Billy was the first one that ever came because of an invitation I sent via Twitter. He was in town for a long weekend performing his standup comedy at a club in Phoenix, and I tweeted an invite to him. Being that we are both from the Pittsburgh area and we offer some Pittsburgh foodie favorites, I thought he might like a taste of some home cooking and our cozy little diner.

I always tweet-invited any celebrities performing in the valley and any sitting or former U.S. presidents, but Billy was the first to accept! I was standing outside by the front door, waiting for Billy to arrive. As he exited his car, he waved to me, and as he walked toward me, smiled, and said, "How about one of those famous hugs." We hugged, and he introduced me to a fellow comic he brought with him. We all walked inside the restaurant like we were old friends. He sat in a booth with his back to the front door. He and his friend ordered a lot of food and enjoyed all of it. While we were visiting with Billy, a customer walked in and sat two booths behind Billy's. When I brought

Billy Gardell with me and my wife, Cyndee

the new customer his order, he said to me, "That guy in the other booth sounds just like Billy Gardell." I said, "You won't believe it, but he looks just like him too." When I went back to sit with Billy, I told him what the customer said, and Billy asked if the customer had any more food coming out. I said, "Yes, a milkshake," and Billy said, "Let me deliver it to him." You can imagine the look on the customer's face when the guy he thought sounded like Billy Gardell *was* Billy Gardell, and he was delivering his milkshake. They chatted for a moment, took a few pics together, and Billy couldn't have been any more gracious. The two comics spent almost two hours eating and visiting with us. He kindly answered all the many questions we had about why the show ended and about the actors he worked with. He told us about an upcoming pilot he was working on, a series, "Bob Hearts Abishola." Before he left, he asked if we would like to come to his show, and we said that we'd love to. He took out his phone, called the box office, and left four tickets for us at the will call.

I was aware of the price of the tickets that he reserved for us: $60 each (his check was $68).

When he asked for his check, I said, "Let's call it even; you got to enjoy our food, we get to see your show." He smiled and, while looking me in the eyes, said, "That's kind of you, but this is your business, and I always pay for my food." I quickly replied, "Not this time. It's on me today." As he got up to leave, we all hugged, took some pics, and I said, "We'll see you at your show." As we cleaned his table, he left a very generous tip under his plate, which more than covered the price of their meals. He's just a regular guy who happens to work in the entertainment business, and he's never forgotten his roots or the people that have allowed him the celebrity status he so humbly lives.

However, my first opportunity to meet and serve up some good grub to a celebrity was one of my most unforgettable experiences. It was at my first restaurant called *Pittsburgh Willy's*. It opened in November of 2008 and was located inside a large antique mall. There were only three tables then, and we only served from 11 a.m. to 3 p.m. One Saturday afternoon, a gentleman wearing blue jeans, a white T-shirt, and sunglasses walked in. He also had a baseball cap that he wore tilted down and used a cane to steady himself. He sat at the table closest to my cash register, along with a young lady that accompanied him.

I walked to their table, gave them menus, and then asked if I could get them a drink. She said, "Just two waters." I delivered their waters, and the gentleman said thank you. I immediately knew that voice but left them to peruse the menu. The young lady came to the counter and gave me their order. When I delivered their food, again the man said thank you, and I again knew that voice. Before I walked away, I said to the gentleman, "You probably get this all the time, but your voice sounds just like Morgan Freeman."

He then tipped the bill of his hat up, looked at me, and said with a smile, "And there's a very good reason for that."

It *was* Morgan Freeman!

He was still using the cane from the terrible automobile accident he had in 2008. I learned he was in town for a Muhammed Ali fundraiser, and he shared that a family member referred him to my tiny restaurant. I wanted to call everyone and tell them that he was at my restaurant, but he obviously was being low-key, evidenced by his sunglasses and ballcap tilted to help cover his face. So, I sat on my hands and respected his apparent choice for anonymity.

While that was an amazing moment for me, it was another actor I met several years later that led to both a friendship and huge respect for the personal journey of Chris Browning.

Chris Browning is most likely an actor you've seen in many movies and television shows and never knew his name. He describes himself on his Instagram account as "That guy who died in that movie you like." Chris is one of Hollywood's busiest actors and the very proud father of three girls. He lives a very balanced life between acting and as a very hands-on daddy. He fills both his Facebook page and Instagram accounts with videos of him with his daughters. Chris is tall, with rugged leading-man good looks, but he most often plays the bad guy you really, really, dislike. He's done many commercial voice-overs, along with major motion pictures and television roles. He also supports small independent filmmakers by offering to work in their films, often gratis.

I met Chris when he was in town shooting a feature film, and the entire cast and crew were staying at a resort just up the street from my restaurant. Chris walked into the restaurant and

Chris Browning and I at Wimpy's, during the filming of his movie

approached the counter. I greeted him and asked him if he wanted to see a menu, but he said he just wanted a drink. I told him that all our drinks were in the coolers to your left. He chose his drink, paid, and sat down at the table closest to the counter. Never having seen him before, I asked him if he lived in the area. He said, "No, I'm in town working." I asked what kind of work he did, and he said, "I'm working on a movie that's being made nearby."

He seemed as though he was hesitant to share exactly what his involvement in the movie was, and as I would soon learn, I misjudged his humility for vagueness. I was now very interested in hearing what this tall, soft-spoken man with a commanding voice was doing. He finally told me he was an actor. I asked him his name, and when he answered, I realized I had never heard of him. I was soon to learn that I'd seen him and heard his voice many times.

We spent nearly two hours talking about just regular stuff, our families, our pasts, and our connection as Pittsburgh Steeler fans. He felt comfortable enough to share a little about his years as an addict, living on the street, fighting his demons, and after five years, taking back his life! Realizing he had been given a second chance, he spent the next 13 years rebuilding both his acting career and personal life. I asked him if he was in any recent T.V. shows I might have seen, and he said he played the character "Gogo" in season five of *Sons of Anarchy*. I had never watched that series but knew that my daughter Kelly had. Kelly was back in the kitchen all the while Chris and I had been chatting, and I walked back to tell her about Chris. I'll never forget our conversation.

I said to her, "Have you ever heard of Gogo, from the…" and she cut me off saying, "from *Sons of Anarchy*?" "Yes," I responded, and she said, "They killed him." And I said, "Well, he's sitting in our restaurant right now." She had that look of, *REALLY*? Then followed me out and talked with Chris for a while. He shared some of the inside scoops about the show and some of the characters.

Kelly and I really enjoyed talking with him and remarked later just how easy he was to chat with. After several hours, Chris said he had to get back to work, as they were shooting some nighttime scenes. Before he left, he asked if we could keep in touch. He said that "in my work and where I live, (near Hollywood) you sometimes never know who your real friends are." It's a business where developing true friendships can be hard. Chris said that he loved how real my daughter and I were. We exchanged phone numbers and hugs. Then that tall, tough-looking stranger that walked in just a few hours before, left as a friend — no, more like family.

We keep in touch through texts and occasional phone calls. He loves playing baseball, and at 57 years old, his passion for playing the game is as strong as ever. I've been to a few of his games when he plays here in Arizona.

I've told Chris that one day, in a future film, he will get an Oscar nomination, and when he does, he must invite me as his guest. That would be the only way I could forgive Chris for not bringing fellow actor Natasha Henstridge into my restaurant.

I didn't know it at the time that she was also in the movie. I learned that in a phone call with Chris a few months later when he told me he did bring Natasha to the restaurant, but we had closed for the evening. I missed my chance to meet the one actress I've had a crush on since I saw her in the movie *Species* (released in 1995). Chris and Natasha first met while filming this movie and have become very close friends. So, my fingers are crossed that I may still get to meet her one day, maybe at the Oscars to watch Chris win best actor!

***To learn more about the fascinating life of Chris Browning and the journey that brought him to where he is today, Google his name, and you'll find his body of work in both film and television. You will also find podcasts and interviews that reveal his struggles overcoming addiction on YouTube. I'm sure you will find his story inspiring and a testimony to the resilience of the human spirit.

HAMBURGERS, HOT DOGS, AND HUGS

"Are Weddings on the Menu?"

or

How I Became "Reverend Randy"

I often felt that I had a spiritual connection with many of my customers. In fact, as mentioned in an earlier chapter, a friend once referred to my restaurant as a ministry. Little did I know that one day, I would be asked to officiate at the weddings of several of my customers, and "Reverend Randy" would become a part of the ministry. Each wedding provided wonderful memories along with unique preparation and planning. Each served to remind me that marriage is not defined by what society considers acceptable or traditional but by who you choose to love.

One day, longtime friends, Lori and Jana, stopped in for lunch to ask me a very important question. I sat with them after they finished lunch, and they asked me if I would do them the honor of officiating their wedding. I had never officiated a wedding or even thought about it. I told them it would be an honor, but how could I legally marry you? They both got big grins on their faces and told me that they had already taken the steps that would legally allow me to become a credentialed minister and marry them! I was so incredibly humbled and immediately said, "Yes!" A few weeks later, I received my official certification from the Universal Life Church.

I was now legally ordained to perform weddings.

Lori Lyford and Jana Gutenson
September 2, 2017

Their wedding was held in a beautiful reception area in the back of San Tan Brewery, a historic building in downtown Chandler Az, just a few doors down from *Wimpy's Paradise.*

Despite my first-time jitters, Lori and Jana's calm and reassuring demeanor made them the perfect couple to introduce me to performing weddings. It was such a warm feeling after they both said, "I do," to have them turn to family and friends and pronounce them a married couple. At the time, I thought, "This is going to be my only time officiating a wedding."

I had never imagined that over the next few years I would marry six more of my customers. Knowing that several couples would want me to not only be part of such a special life moment but to officiate the event was an honor that I would cherish forever.

Who would have thought that the Elvis Memorial Chapel in Apache Junction — a movie prop from the 1969 Elvis Presley movie "Charro!"

— would provide the next backdrop for the wedding of friends Doug and Jenn? It was a unique wedding with not only a historic setting but lent itself to playfulness, as shown by the hot dog tie the bride and groom purchased for me and insisted that I wear!

Douglas Mitchell and
Jenny Sylvester-Mitchell
February 18, 2018

The Elvis Memorial Chapel

However, one of the most unforgettable weddings I officiated was not a customer request but from someone who read a Facebook post about one of the weddings I officiated. The couple to be married contacted me in a quiet panic. The bride's father was in the ICU at a local hospital and not doing well. They wanted him to be part of the wedding. They worked with the hospital to get permission for several family members to be present but received word the day before the wedding that the hospital chaplain would not be available to officiate. The bride-to-be remembered seeing my post and contacted me early on the morning of the wedding. I told her I would be honored to do it. I had no idea what to expect and very little time to prepare, but I felt that God had prepared me through the previous weddings for exactly this moment.

The ICU staff provided all the decorations. There was a cake and punch and about ten family members on hand. Standing at the foot of the bed, I began the ceremony — the groom on one side of the bed, the bride on the other side. I wanted to actively include the father in the ceremony, but he was bedridden, very weak, and unable to speak. I saw him grasping his daughter's hand and his fingers slightly opening and closing before the ceremony began.

Since the tradition of the dad walking his daughter down the aisle wasn't possible, I spoke to the dad alone for a moment and whispered into his

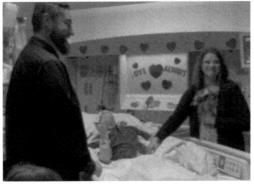

ear, asking if he could make a thumbs up fist. He answered me by making one, and he smiled.

Shannon and Jeff Mrantz November 16, 2019

Harkening back to old marriage traditions, I decided to ask the bride's father if he was giving his blessing for the marriage that was about to happen. It was a moment of complete silence, and all eyes were on the father. It was then followed by collective smiles and happy reactions as one hand grasped his daughter's hand while the other gave a firm thumbs up! The ceremony was quick, the emotions high, and it was a very beautiful moment that I will never forget! I left shortly after to allow the family alone time to celebrate.

As I drove back home, I realized how blessed I was and how once again it was the heart and passion of my restaurant, not the food, that allowed this moment to happen. And I knew my dad was smiling down on me and giving me a big thumbs up!

Dan and Tiffany Vandenbergh
with Dan's boys, Max, Drew,
and Rudy
December 15, 2018

Zack Coffman and
Rachel Murdoch-Coffman
January 13, 2018

Tanner and Alissa Lopez-McClure
March 5, 2019

Steve Skigis and
Rita Kline-Skigis
April 21, 2018
While the officiating of Steve and Rita's wedding was a huge privilege, Rita said, "Our friendship had gone full circle when you accompanied me to the mortuary to make final arrangements after Steve had passed from cancer on November 11, 2020."

Scott and Jennifer Rosato
October 21, 2017

106

"Where's My Milkshake?"

or

How Kindness and a Milkshake Eased a Broken Heart

Shortly after I opened my first restaurant in 2008, I learned that not every customer that walked through the door was there for our home-cooked food. Many came seeking comfort: The comfort that comes when you sit among others, enjoying good food, laughter, and those typical diner sounds. Just people sharing a fun experience, knowing that if you are sitting alone at your table, you're still part of the collective group, dining at that moment.

That people came to restaurants for reasons other than filling their bellies was what I shared with every employee. And that every customer has a story, and whatever life handed them on any given day can affect their behavior. So, when you get that surly, angry, distant, or flat-out rude customer, always remember that they have a story. We are given the opportunity to show that customer kindness, love, and compassion, along with serving them amazing comfort food.

One late Friday afternoon, during our normal slow time between the lunch rush and dinner service, I got my most amazing opportunity yet to practice what I preached to my employees. I was sitting at our cashier's counter doing some doodling when the front door opened and in stepped an older gentleman, thin and slightly hunched over. He had a full head of wavy gray hair, a white dress shirt with the collar opened, and a thin black tie, swinging loosely as he slowly lumbered toward me. Black pants and a black fedora held in front of him completed the look. I reached for a menu and greeted him with a friendly, "Welcome to *Wimpy's Paradise*, sir," to which he gave no reply. He sat with his back to me, placed his fedora on the seat next to him, and put both hands, open-palmed, over his eyes and let out a very pronounced sigh. As I made my way to his table, I set the menu in front of him and asked if he'd eaten here before. His reply was, "Give me a hamburger, no cheese." His hands still covered his face. "Anything to drink, sir?," I asked, and again in a short, gruff answer, he said, "NO!" Of all the customers that I had experienced, I sensed the gentleman was making it quite clear that he wanted no small talk, just a burger, no cheese.

I took his ticket back to the kitchen, repeated to the cook, "Burger, no cheese," and returned to sit at the cashier's counter. The gentleman's back was to me, and I studied his behavior. He was softly strumming his fingers on the tabletop and quietly mumbling to himself. At times, he would look across the table, then give a heavy sigh and lower his eyes to his busy fingers. I felt so helpless, and I wanted to speak with him to see if I could, in some small way, cheer him up. However, he made it abundantly clear that he didn't want to be bothered.

Then, the order-up bell rang from the kitchen, and I picked up the burger, utensils, and napkin and started towards my only customer. He leaned back as I set his burger, silverware, and napkin down, and I asked him if there was anything else that I could get him. Without looking up at me, he said angrily, "Where's my milkshake?"

He had never ordered a milkshake, but I said to him, "Sir, I forgot what flavor shake you ordered." "Chocolate!" he yelled back. So, I walked away to make him a chocolate shake. I brought him his shake in our traditional milkshake glass, which was a tall, old-fashioned soda fountain glass.

I was soon going to find out just how important that presentation was to him. "Here's your shake, sir," I said as I set it on his table. He reached for it and said nothing. I stepped away, uncertain if I would ever be able to show this gentleman any light or hope in what seemed to be a dark day for him. I watched as he slowly finished his burger and ever so slowly got to the bottom of the shake. Then, I heard the sound that we all love to hear: the straw sucking the last of that delicious chocolate shake. That was my signal. Time to accept the fact that sometimes, people may not be ready to see the light at that moment. Sometimes, they just want to be left to process and deal with whatever is hurting them, or maybe, just maybe, he was comfortable in being a private, surly, angry old man.

As I brought the man his check, I told him that I didn't charge him for the milkshake since it was my fault that I "forgot" which flavor he had ordered. I asked him how his burger was, and for the first time, he looked up at me. His eyes were bloodshot and watery. He gave me a little smile and said, "My wife would have loved this place." It was then that I had a glimpse into this man's story. I asked if I could sit down at the table. "Please do," he responded. I asked him, already knowing the answer, "Where's your wife?" Our eyes met, and he said, "I just buried her, and it was just me and our pastor. In fact, this is my first meal without her in

55 years." I was now feeling a hint of his pain. "Please tell me about your wife," and for the next thirty minutes, he shared their love story, which included their first date, where they shared a chocolate shake.

As he stood to leave, we hugged, and he thanked me for the meal. As he turned to walk away, he said, "I love your place, but you do understand that I can never come back here." I replied, "I understand." His parting words were, "I will never forget your kindness or our chocolate shake."

The Man in the Van

or

How Chicken Soup May Have Made a Difference

It was late September 2016, at approximately 2 p.m. Our restaurant, *Wimpy's Paradise*, was closed on Mondays, but this day, my wife Cyndee and I were at the restaurant doing some heavy cleaning. The lights were off, but we left the front door open in case anyone wanted to buy a cold drink or stop in for a hug!

A van pulled up and parked directly in front of our store. I watched as a woman got out on the passenger side while the driver stayed in the van. She stood in front of the restaurant, seemingly hesitant to walk in, just stood there clutching her purse. She noticed our front door was slightly open and cautiously walked in. "Are you open?" she asked. I replied, "Just for cold drinks." As she walked toward the coolers, she asked, "Do you have ginger ale?" "We do," I said, and she grabbed a cold can of Canada Dry. She then shared what brought her and her husband to our front door that day.

Every year for the past several years, they took a few months to drive across the country and spend time at each of their children's homes. They loved spending time visiting grandkids and having weeks to spend at each stop. But this trip, we learned, was their final one. It was, as she said, their "goodbye tour." Her husband was diagnosed with stage 4 blood cancer. He was given less than a year to live, so they decided to do what they always did in the summer. Take a road trip and hope her husband wouldn't be worse for the wear. They stopped here to shop for some unique southwestern gifts at Sibley's West, a gift shop three doors down from my restaurant. But her husband was too weak to walk with her and stayed in the van. He recently was having trouble keeping food down, and ginger ale seemed to help with his nausea. She was soft-spoken but strong-willed and was going to shop on her own. I watched her deliver the soda to her husband and then walk to the gift shop. I had an idea.

Shortly after I opened *Pittsburgh Willy's*, a dear friend of mine mentioned she had just made her chicken and wild rice healing soup. I was looking for a signature soup for our menu and was intrigued by both her recipe and the name. She graciously offered to share her recipe, and it became one of our most popular menu items. Now, while neither she nor I made any claims that her soup really healed anyone, I kept the complete name, and I will let you decide what this soup may or may not have done to help this man with stage 4 cancer.

As I thought about the man in the van, I asked my wife if we should take some of our soup out to the husband. We both agreed it sure couldn't hurt. I heated an 8-ounce cup and delivered it to him. I gave him extra napkins and two small plastic bags in case he couldn't keep it down. He thanked me profusely and blessed me as I walked away. We watched him from back in the restaurant, and he quickly devoured the soup, even tilting the cup back to sip all the remaining broth. I then saw him step out of the van and sit at a table in front of our restaurant. I asked him if he would like another cup of soup? He replied enthusiastically, "I sure would." I brought him a second cup, and he finished it as quickly as the first. Cyndee and I got busy cleaning, and when we next looked to check on the man, he was gone. He wasn't at the table or in the van!

We kept busy until we again heard the front door open. In walked both the lady and her husband. She wanted to thank us for the soups and soda and tell us that her husband walked by himself to where she was shopping. He also hadn't walked that far in months without assistance. He was keeping the soup down and ready to drive. We hugged them, gave them some bottles of water, and watched as they drove away. For the next year, Cyndee and I often wondered how their "goodbye tour" went and if the gentleman was still alive.

We got a most wonderful answer to our questions when about one year later, they both walked into the restaurant. He had gained weight and walked with ease. His oncologist said he was showing remarkable improvement, and while remission is rare with stage 4 blood cancer, he was, for now, able to live a full life without the ravages his body was fighting a year ago. They purposely stopped to see us on the first leg of their annual road trip. This one they called "the bonus tour." They wanted to thank us for last year's hospitality and share with us the husband's miraculous recovery — and to purchase some of our Stacey's chicken and wild rice soup to take on the road with them! I told them when it comes to that soup, your money is no good here. We sent them off with two quarts of soup and two big hugs.

I retired and closed the restaurant before their 2018 trip. We can only pray they are still taking their bonus trips and wonder if Stacey's chicken and wild rice soup played a role in his remarkable recovery.

Stacey's Chicken & Wild Rice Healing Soup Recipe

1 cup sweet onion, chopped

2 tbsp minced garlic

1 whole roasted chicken (Costco/Sam's) save drippings in a tray

One of each - red, green, yellow pepper (large diced)

1 small bunch of celery (cut in thin slices)

2 large carrots (cut in half lengthwise & sliced thin)

1 bunch of chopped Italian parsley

1 box of Rice-a-Roni (or available brand) Long Grain and Wild Rice

(seasoning packet is also used)

2 packets of Good Seasons Italian salad dressing mix, 1 reg. 1 zesty

5 boxes chicken broth (32 oz)

1/3 cup of wild rice

8 oz of water

3 tbsp of virgin olive oil

2 tbsp sugar

1 tbsp Tony Chachere's Cajun seasoning (or similar) add to taste
1 tsp salt
1 tsp pepper
14.5 oz. can diced tomatoes
Fresh lemon & grated asiago cheese (optional to add when serving)

Cut all veggies and set them aside. In a large stockpot, add minced garlic, chopped onions, and olive oil. Stir on med heat until onions and garlic are sauteed (slightly browned). (2-3 minutes).

Then add 4 boxes of broth and 8 oz of water to the pot while stirring the garlic and onions. Bring to a near boil and add sugar, salt, and pepper, wild rice, the box of Rice-a-Roni, and seasoning packet. Add Cajun seasoning.

Add all cut veggies and Italian parsley, bring to a boil for a few minutes, then reduce heat. Add canned tomatoes and the pulled chicken (skin removed) and add drippings from the tray. Let everything simmer for about 30 minutes. If it's too thick, add another box of broth.

Add Cajun seasoning to taste when serving and serve with a drizzle of freshly squeezed lemon and grated Asiago cheese.

Makes 6-8 quarts…great for sharing.

It also makes a great breakfast burrito. Drain the broth, scramble with eggs and cheese and roll in a tortilla.

Enjoy!

Here a Sign, There a Sign, Everywhere a Sign

or

How a Sign Can Touch Your Heart and Soul

I started putting signs out in front of my restaurant the first year I opened *Pittsburgh Willy's*. The original sign was a simple welcome by the front door. I would sometimes change it to make it topical, and customers all responded favorably. In fact, my regulars would look forward to reading and commenting on them, many asking me to change them more frequently. But it wasn't until I opened my restaurant three miles south in historic downtown Chandler that my signs started being photographed and caught the attention of local media. I put my first A-frame sign outside my new restaurant a week after I opened on February 14, 2013. Like all my signs, it was written by me, by hand, and from the heart, meaning I was *ONLY* concerned about the message and not the content being written perfectly. In fact, my less than neat handwriting and often whimsical, topical, and sometimes serious messages became a favorite photo op for those walking by. We were located just about 50 yards from the historic San Marcos Hotel, which brought a lot of worldwide travelers to my restaurant and the signs. I would watch people walking by stop, read the current A-frame sign, then snap a picture. Many would then come in to eat, buy a drink, or get an ice cream. It became clear that my outdoor signs were bringing in customers and creating a buzz.

I originally created my signs to bring in potential customers walking past the restaurant with menu specials. It was also where I introduced the offer that ANYONE could simply come in for a FREE hug, no purchase necessary. I could never have imagined that it was the Free Hug offer that would draw the most interest, and unexpectedly, the media's attention. After my first A-frame, I realized

I could write two different messages, one on each side, thereby doubling my opportunity to share daily menu specials along with topical and often whimsical comments. It wasn't long before my street signs became a photo op for many, a brand builder for the restaurant, and a huge attention grabber for local media. One sign even went international!

The sign that garnered international attention was devoted totally as a response to the palpable division in our country in early 2016. I always took pride in welcoming anyone in my restaurant, and I wanted anyone who felt marginalized or fearful to know they were always welcome and safe at *Wimpy's Paradise.*

What first alerted me to the attention this sign was getting were the crowds of people stopping to photograph it.

I started receiving phone calls from local news stations wanting to come and do a story on the sign. There were two live remotes and several other media stories about the sign. It was now becoming a must-see for people visiting downtown Chandler, but more importantly, the message was resonating with a lot of people.   One afternoon, I was sitting behind the cash register, watching customers enjoying their lunch, when I noticed a gentleman outside reading the sign. He stood still, hands clasped behind his back, just staring at the sign. After a few moments, he turned and looked inside the restaurant, then slowly approached the front door. He laid a hand on the door to push it open but stood there for a moment, seeming uncertain if he wanted to walk in.

Eventually, he pushed open the door and walked directly toward where I was sitting. He asked in a voice that was slightly trembling, "Are you the one who wrote the sign?" I told him, yes, and he asked if he could get a hug? I stood up, walked to him, and we hugged. He was very slight and thin, but his hug was powerful. Once we ended the hug, he stepped back and, through tears told me how thankful he was to see that sign and to meet and hug me.

He explained that both his wife and adult daughter wear traditional Muslim clothes, where they are always fully covered. He then said, "My daughter will be here visiting us soon. I would like to bring them both here to meet you and see the sign." "I'd be honored," I replied, and we embraced again. Then he shared the importance of that sign to him. He said he and his wife had received hurtful and verbally abusive comments from strangers while just simply walking by them. They had also been refused service at some businesses. He said seeing that sign gave him hope and made him feel welcomed and respected. He wanted to share it with his family and friends.

A few weeks later, he walked in with his wife and daughter, and this time he was smiling. As he introduced me to his family, I extended my arms to hug his wife; he quickly raised his arm in front of me, and his wife stepped back. He explained that in their culture, it's not appropriate to hug his wife and daughter. I respectfully backed up and we shook hands. I was thankful that I had just learned something new about their customs. It brought us closer and reminded me how, with all our differences, we can and must respect the accepted social norms of all people. Too often, its fear, driven by ignorance that manifests itself in violence toward others. Hopefully, we can all learn more about those around us who dress, worship, speak and celebrate differently. Realizing we ALL share a heartbeat and a desire to love and be loved, feel safe, and be accepted.

"Here's Your Sign!"

128

Muffins with Muslims

or

How I Came to Embrace the Muslim Community

I didn't have any contacts with Muslims in my youth that I knew of. In fact, I didn't meet anyone who was Muslim till 1995 at age 42, again, that I knew of. His name was Safet, and he was a co-worker who relocated to Arizona from Bosnia during an armed conflict that saw over 100,000 Bosnians killed. He spoke no English when he arrived here. He was supported by and stayed with other Bosnians that helped him come to this country. He learned and quickly mastered air conditioning and heating repair skills, and he studied daily to learn the English language. He'd only been in this country for about two years when we met. From the first day we worked together, I felt a quiet yet confident strength about him. He was a big strapping guy with large hands, a strong grip, and a willingness to learn more and help his workmates. We quickly became close friends and remain so 26 years later. His English is still a bit rough, his accent still thick, and his way of saying common American phrases is simply refreshing. For instance, on a phone call, I said something to which he replied, "Wait till I see you four eyes." Which was his way of saying face-to-face. His sense of humor was wicked, and his quick responses, hysterical. I remember one time I was teasing him about his use of the letters V and W. He would say vindow, and wacuum. I would say, "So, if you can say the letters V and W, why can't you say window and vacuum?" He looked at me, smiled, and said, "Don't vorry about it." And that was my first Muslim friend, but thankfully, not my last.

Once my standing offer for free hugs started getting lots of media attention, I got to meet and hug over 5,000 people in the ten years I owned my restaurants. While I can't remember every hug, I can certainly remember several of the people that I hugged that made a profound impact on me. Two of those people were Tara and Deedra, both born in America but who converted to Islam as young adults. Our first meeting was both funny and educational. I was sitting behind my register with no customers at the time, and suddenly the front door pushed open. In walked three ladies, all wearing headscarves and smiling from ear to ear. My immediate thought was, what am I going to feed them? In my total ignorance of Muslim culture, I assumed they only ate Mediterranean-style foods like hummus, olives, grape leaves, and pita bread. All I had was hot dogs and burgers! Boy, was I about to have a teaching moment!

As they got within hugging distance, they said they read a newspaper article about my hugs and wanted to meet me and get a hug. We hugged and smiled and just felt an instant connection. For the next three hours we sat and talked, got to know each other, and we ate! Since my hot dogs were all beef, they enjoyed both hot dogs and hamburgers, and I learned that except for pork products, all foods were on the table. Tara was just starting a business that was born from a passion to spread love and kindness. It was called the *Love Glasses Revolution*. She sold heart-shaped glasses with the attached slogan "Choosing to see the world through love." She has since seen her business explode, gaining national exposure and recognition. Along with selling Love Glasses, she has gifted hundreds of pairs throughout the world.

Deedra had a career as an immigration attorney and has run for the U.S. Senate and the Maricopa County Board of Supervisors. Deedra has written a very fun and enlightening book about her times on the campaign trail with her best friend, Tara. It's called "Campaign Chronicles," and it recounts the many conversations she shared while traveling throughout the state during her campaign.

Tara and Deedra have become my very close and dear friends. I've learned a lot about Islam and about the over one billion peace-loving people who practice it. I held some events at my restaurant called Muffins with Muslims, where everyone was welcome to bring questions and hopefully gain a better understanding of the Muslim culture.

I believe we ALL have the responsibility to take the time to learn about and understand those that dress and worship differently than us. I sent personal invites to my friends, some of whom I knew thought that all Muslims were evil and wanted to infiltrate America to ultimately destroy it. All I was hoping for was that they would attend with their currently held beliefs, bring a somewhat open mind, and be willing to challenge themselves by asking questions and simply spending time with a few Muslims.

Tara, Deedra, and a few other Muslims were on hand, and they made it abundantly clear that they welcomed ALL questions concerning Islam, Muslims, and Sharia law. We shared two hours of wonderful conversation, but not a single friend that feared Muslims showed up. I can only assume that they preferred to live with their unchallenged beliefs about Muslims, learned from "news" sources that fed into their fear and hate.

As for me, I learned that as with any group of people, be it race, color, religion, or political affiliation; we often use a broad brush to unfairly form our opinions. All groups have those that engage in behavior that is both horrific and contradictory to the beliefs and behavior of the majority. I encourage everyone to Look, Listen and Learn about others before we share misinformation or express words that could very well be 100 percent incorrect and bring harm to innocent people.

Trading Ham for Bacon

or

How a Good Deed Became Lessons in Dignity and Respect

In the downtown area of any city, there will always be people experiencing homelessness. Some set up tents, sleep behind bushes, or find shelter in alleyways. I would often feed them with money donated by my customers in a "pay-it-forward fund" that a customer suggested we start. One Sunday morning, I had just delivered a plate of food to a homeless gentleman on our patio. As I walked away from his table, I heard a voice behind me ask, "Do you feed homeless people for free?" I turned to see a tall, thin man looking tired and worn. "Yes, we do," I said. "May I have breakfast?" he asked. "Of course," I replied and offered him a seat at an empty table. He quickly added, "Can I get it to go?"

I returned a few minutes later with a breakfast of ham, potatoes, scrambled eggs, and toast, the same breakfast we prepared for all the homeless customers, only this one packaged to go. He opened it, and while looking down at the food, said, without raising his head, "Can I trade the ham for bacon?" My first thought was that the adage "beggars can't be choosers" wasn't true! But what I really learned was that while I was feeding someone that didn't have the means to pay, I wasn't serving him with the same respect and quality service that I dedicated myself and my staff to provide to all customers. I didn't offer him a menu where he could select his breakfast of choice, like every other customer. I was being paid for this breakfast from our customer-created fund, but I was failing miserably in the importance of treating everyone equally and with dignity.

That simple request to replace the ham with bacon taught me so much. I learned from those seven words that while my intentions were well-meant, by not providing EVERY customer the same dining experience, I was unwittingly discriminating against the very customers that I felt so blessed to be able to serve.

I returned with his to-go container with three strips of bacon on top of the ham. He thanked me for adding the bacon and said, "Bless you, sir," shook my hand, and walked away to wherever he was going to enjoy his breakfast.

I never saw him again but thought of him whenever we served another customer who didn't have the means to pay while they looked over the menu and decided what they wanted to order.

There was another moment with a woman and her dog that left a lasting impression on me. I was sitting outside my restaurant one evening, and this woman came up to the door and peered inside.

 I said, "Are you and your dog hungry?" "No," she said, "but can I look at your albums and play one?" We had a record player and albums that our customers

could browse through and play. "Of course, you can," I said. She leafed through the albums and seemed to enjoy the memories associated with them. Well, what album did she play? Surprisingly, she didn't play any but thanked me for a trip down memory lane.

Over the years, I was proud that we provided a place for those who needed comfort, a meal, or just a safe place to rest. I think the Facebook comment that I received when we announced that we were closing says it best.

Dan
Darn.... Wimpys is done? Real bummer.... You are, and were one of the only places in the country that treated me as a human being, and not just some bum.... Thank you for that!!!!

20m   Like   Reply   ♡1

I Beat the BEAR

or

How Covid-19 Earned a Chapter in This Book

It was mid-January of 2021, and I had just been tested for COVID-19. Most of my immediate family had recently tested positive but only had minor symptoms. I hadn't written a single word on this book since November 17, 2020, after my son-in-law Brice's sudden passing. Now COVID-19 was about to shelve any writing plans for the next seven months.

Once I was hospitalized with COVID-19, I decided to do a daily Facebook journal along with an occasional video. My intent with the journal and videos was twofold.

1. Bring real-time information to anyone following me as to what the daily struggles are for those that become hospitalized with COVID-19.

2. To keep me focused and break the sadness and angst of being isolated from family and friends.

I really wanted to show the raw reality of what suffering with and possibly even dying from COVID-19 was like. I couldn't know when or if there would be a final journal entry because I might not recover, or I could be walking out of the hospital having survived the ravages of COVID-19.

From this point on, I will refer to COVID-19 as the BEAR. Why? Because like all mass murderers, it's the victims' names that should be remembered, not their killers. I also wanted to give everyone a visual of what the virus was to me. It was like a powerful "BEAR" that hibernates silently within you, but once it awakens, it can viciously tear at you. It will attack ANY weakness it can exploit to satisfy its own voracious hunger to thrive while permanently damaging or destroying any of the body's organs, and if it can, it will kill you.

It was my fourth day after testing positive for the BEAR. Just a few days before, I received a surprise delivery. It was a pulse oximeter. It slides over a finger and reads both your pulse rate and oxygen level in your blood. It is the single most important tool anyone can use to know when they need to get to the E.R. My dear friend Heidi Ross mailed me one out of concern for my high risk for the BEAR. That act of kindness may have saved my life. I had some slight respiratory issues for a few days, nothing too severe. I also had an on and off low-grade fever, and I just felt punky.

While I decided to take a bath and just relax, my wife phoned my two daughters to update them on how I was feeling. As I sat in the tub, I put the pulse oximeter on my finger, and it read 110 for my pulse and 82 for my O2 concentration. I knew it was supposed to be in the high 90s, but I just figured I'd wait and see how it goes. I did call out to my wife and tell her what it read. She walked into the bathroom to tell me that your daughters said, "Get to the hospital NOW." So, I did!

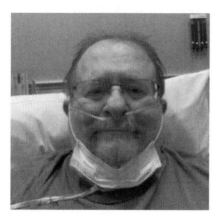

E.R. arrival January 17, 2020

The E.R. was not busy at all. I was taken immediately to the back and placed on a gurney in a treatment room. I had both nurses and doctors caring for me the moment I was settled.

My temperature at that point was 102, and I still felt OK, but my anxiety was quickly increasing. After chest X-rays, a CT scan, and blood work, I was told I was going to be admitted when a room became available. The BEAR was awake and had a hold on me!

It wasn't until Monday morning, 36 hours after I arrived at the hospital, that I was taken to my room. As they rolled me through the halls of the E.R., I witnessed a deeply disturbing sight.

Every room was occupied, and stretcher after stretcher lined the hallways. There was only a portable rolling curtain affording patients little if any privacy or dignity. Most I would learn had been attacked by the BEAR. The moaning and crying I heard is something I will never forget. In just 36 hours, the relatively slow E.R. had turned into an overflowing triage center of pain and suffering.

When I arrived at my room, I was lifted from the stretcher to my bed, and it was the beginning of the most intense 20 days of my life!

Nurses took my vital signs and blood work and removed my nasal cannula and replaced it with an oxygen mask. Members of several medical disciplines came into my room throughout the day. They explained in detail what would be included in my care and treatment. The first thing I was given was a simple yet very important piece of medical equipment, the spirometer. It's a little closed pump system with a tube attached. You inhale into the tube after you've exhaled and it measures ventilation, which is the movement of air in and out of the lungs. It is literally an apparatus that can help

YOU, the patient, assist greatly in possibly saving your own life. Using it as directed helps strengthen your lungs. I found it very difficult at first to move the measurement gauge. Using it really exhausted me, so I didn't use it as often as my doctor ordered, until the most terrifying night of my life.

It was pretty much the same routine from day one of admission until day three. Drawing blood four times a day and respiratory therapy checked my oxygen needs. Doctors updated me on my progress, I had my room cleaned, and lots of medications, both oral and through the several IVs running through my veins. My breathing was becoming labored, and I was about to learn how the BEAR was just biding its time, waiting to attack!

I had a big window in my room that faced west, and I could see the beautiful mountains in the distance and watch the sunsets. My favorite ritual since I retired is to wake up before sunrise, grab a coffee and sit in my Paul Bunyan rocker on our front porch and watch the sunrise. Hearing the silence beautifully interrupted by the waking birds' first chirps of the day, along with the many other sounds unique to morning were comforting to me. Those sounds remind us that our world is waking up. I still enjoyed the sunset from my room, but I missed those simple, quiet mornings on the porch, gently rocking, sipping my coffee, and breathing that crisp fresh air.

"Help! Help! Help!" I screamed on the morning of my fourth day in isolation. It was a loud, blood-curdling scream for help. I was doubled over sitting in my bed clutching my side, tears streaming down my face. I couldn't reach for the nurse call button because I was paralyzed in pain — pain like I had never experienced in my 67 years.

The nurses heard my screams for help, gowned up in protective gear, and rushed in. I begged for pain medicine, anything to stop the pain. A doctor soon arrived. He examined me and ordered both strong pain medicines and a CT scan.

Once I was calm, and the pain controlled, I was taken to get my scan. Only an emergency allows an isolated patient to be moved from their room for a test that can't be done bedside. I knew that something serious had just happened but was too drugged up to care at that moment.

The night the Bear attacked my spleen

The results showed that the BEAR had created blood clots that lodged in my spleen, virtually destroying it. I was told I was very lucky that the clots got lodged in my spleen and not in my heart. As my doctor later assured me, "You can live without a spleen."

I rested comfortably for the next ten hours, pumped with pain medication, and monitored closely by the nursing staff. The extreme pain from that event never returned, but I would feel intermittent sharp stabs in the area, painful but manageable. I was settled in bed, the head raised so I was in a sitting position. I'd just taken my evening meds, was physically exhausted from the day's events, and was ready to sleep. Little did I know that in just a few hours I would spend the most terrifying, emotional, and comforting night of my entire 20-day stay and it would forever change me!

I was awakened by a firm knock on my door. As I opened my eyes, I saw someone approach me. I could just see a figure walking toward me, unable to see clearly enough to know exactly who it was. As the figure made it to my bedside, I saw a white lab coat. It was a doctor, one who I'd never seen before. She spoke in a German accent and simply said, "You have to let us know by morning if you want to go on a ventilator or try to fight this yourself." I asked her, "How sick am I?" "Very sick and getting close to maybe needing ventilated." Then just as mysteriously and quietly as she arrived, she turned and walked out, closing the door, and leaving me alone in total darkness.

At that moment, I felt like she was the angel of death. No comforting words, no kindness in her tone, just one straight cold question, and I had never been more terrified in my life!

I couldn't fall back to sleep. I sat in the darkness, thinking I may never see my family, friends, or dog Tilly again. I was fighting an enemy I couldn't see. I was just slipping away, waiting for the next BEAR attack! I turned and kneeled on my bed, tears pouring down my cheeks, my breathing more labored. I was doubled over begging God to take me now. I can't do this anymore. The pain is too great; I just want the pain and misery gone. I whispered through quivering lips, "Please God, take me now, please, I can't fight this anymore." After I begged for God to take me, my thoughts immediately went to my granddaughter Cara.

She was diagnosed with P.O.T.S. (Postural Orthostatic Tachycardia Syndrome) and several other ancillary medical conditions that are often associated with it. She was only 15 when she almost died after a severe loss of blood. Her jugular vein was nicked and cauterized during a surgery. She started bleeding when the scab tore open seven days after having a tonsillectomy. Luckily, her dad was with her and rushed her to the E.R. in time to save her. She had emergency surgery to save her life. It would be one of three times in the next three years that Cara would be moments from death.

In December of 2019, she had to have lifesaving surgery at Phoenix Children's Hospital to remove blood clots near her heart. We all said our goodbyes to her as this rare surgical procedure had a low survival rate. Cara was again at death's door. She survived the surgery and spent seven days on a ventilator. On the seventh day, after they removed her from ventilation, I leaned down toward her and whispered in her ear, "Cara, we've come so close to losing you three times, and you just keep fighting." She looked me in the eyes and whispered in a soft, broken voice, "Papa, I'm hard to kill."

It was that comment and that memory that I thought of as I knelt in my bed, ready to give up my fight with the BEAR. I looked up, knelt up straight, and said out loud, "I can't quit, I can't give up; Cara never quit." It was that moment that I committed to fight the BEAR and do everything in my power to beat it and show it that, like my granddaughter, I too am hard to kill!

I felt a renewed strength, and I adjusted my position in bed. I returned to sitting upright and reached for my spirometer. From that moment on, I would use it every 15 minutes while I was awake. As I finished my breathing treatment, I took a big drink of water, laid my head back, and soon drifted off to sleep.

I slept till I felt a gentle but firm squeeze on my right arm near my bicep. The room was dark, and I turned on a light expecting to see a nurse standing next to me, but there was no one there! I didn't give it much thought. I turned off the light and quickly fell back to sleep.

I don't know how long I'd been sleeping when I again felt a hand laid on the same area, only this one felt firmer, and like the other, it felt the way a loved one would touch you to comfort you and let you know they are there. Like the first touch, when I turned on the lights, no one was there! This time I left the lights on.

I had an undeniable feeling at that moment that I wasn't alone. I felt a calmness and comfort that I hadn't felt since I first arrived in my room.

There was no fear, no angst, just the sounds of silence. I now felt I had both the strength and courage to beat this virus. More importantly, I knew I wasn't alone in this fight, nor was I alone in room 320!

The next morning, for the first time, I started my day with not just breakfast, but with confidence. I told the doctors I was going to do everything I could to assist them in getting me ready to go home, start rehabbing, and move on from the BEAR attack. I spent all but about 6 hours out of bed. I walked over 200 steps a day in my room, sat up in a chair, used my spirometer, and prayed.

My daily journals became more about the positives. It was about how I was now feeling in control and actively doing all I could to not allow the pneumonia to progress. I started sleeping sitting up. My bedside table was raised in front of me, where I would place a pillow on it. Then, I would cross my extended arms in front of me and lay them on the pillow. I would then place another pillow over my arms, resting my head on that pillow. This position opened my lungs to their maximum air exchange. This simple technique helped increase the amount of life-saving oxygen into my lungs.

One morning, I was still asleep in that position in my chair. My doctor walked in and saw me. He gently woke me up and asked if I slept like that all night in the chair. I told him yes, and I prefer sleeping this way most times now because it was easier to breathe this way. He said he would be advising his other patients to try to do the same, when in bed or in a chair, and how that position opens the lungs. He also said my oxygen readings overnight were a lot better, and he would be reducing my oxygen flow.

For the first time since my admission, I felt myself getting stronger, not weaker. I started showering every day and taking measured walks in my room with the respiratory therapist noting my progress. My appetite was back, and I often ordered double entrees with each meal. It would still be two weeks before I was discharged, but I was beating the BEAR and slowly taking back my life.

Starting to feel like my old self

For 20 days, I would have dozens of staff in and out of my room, always wearing protective gowns, gloves, and face protection.

For 20 days, I never saw faces, I only saw eyes, but that's where the nurses showed their feelings, whether they wanted to or not.

After a while, I could see in their eyes when they were burdened with sadness, but they still showed caring compassion for me and always entered my room with a happy greeting. As we became more connected, I learned how most purposely distanced themselves from becoming too close to patients battling the BEAR because so many would lose the fight. The collective grief that grew with each passing was devastating, and there was no end in sight! They shared how they would have to mentally prepare themselves for their shift after a few days off. Before getting their report, they would scan the whiteboard to see if any of their patients' names had been removed. Then with precious little hope, they'd ask if they were discharged home or died.

Those of us who were lucky enough to show improvement and possibly be discharged soon realized our rooms had become a refuge of sorts for the nurses. It sometimes seemed like nurses would gown up, walk in, and do something minimal just to escape the overwhelming sadness and spend time with someone who was responding positively to their hard work and dedication. It was a needed break to help them momentarily escape the heartbreak, suffering, or loss of life caused by the BEAR.

I was beginning to understand just how amazing nurses really are and the depth of their commitment to caring for so many patients, knowing that many would not survive. All the doctors, support staff that provide meals, clean your room, take your blood, and perform the many tests are all selflessly working to save our lives in our battle against the BEAR.

On Thursday, February 4, 2021, I was discharged home, clapped out by many teary-eyed and boisterously happy staff from Dignity General Hospital. I was rolled out in a wheelchair through the same entrance that I walked in 20 days earlier. Oh, I almost forgot to share who it was that touched my arm that terrifying night and comforted me. The first touch was my mother, and the second, my son-in-law Brice, who just passed away ten weeks earlier. How do I know it was them?

A few days later it was confirmed when my friend Jill, who temporarily crossed over several years ago after a horrific car accident, and after making an agreement from a voice on the other side, returned to our world. She has had visions of angels' activities ever since. She told me she had seen both my mom and Brice in my room, and she told me this BEFORE I had ever shared what happened that night. Seems like I wasn't isolated after all for those twenty days in room 320. I was surrounded by angels, working as nurses and doctors, and watched over by my guardian angels, my mother, Carmel, and my son-in-law Brice.

About The Author

Randy Walters is the quintessential guy next door. He, along with his wife Cyndee, have raised two amazing daughters, Kelly and Brynn. He worked hard at several jobs over the years, from an Emergency response E.M.T. to Paramedic at the Arizona state prison, city recreation leader, and finally full-time painter at Chandler AZ Hospital. He attended evening classes at A.S.U. over 8 of those years. He left A.S.U. 18 credits short of his degree in Criminal Justice. But he NEVER gave up his dream to one day open a restaurant.

During 2008's depressed economy and having recently been fired from his hospital painting job, Randy was able to talk his way into opening a very small hot dog joint inside an antique mall in Chandler, Arizona. Randy closed his restaurants in 2018. Now fully retired, Randy has devoted his time to his three granddaughters, Cara, Josslyn, and Natalie, and to writing. Randy is a Love rebel, who spends every day looking for the good in people, supporting those who are marginalized, and offering hugs to anyone that needs or asks for one.

You can contact Randy with questions or comments at ***Damillhunk22@yahoo.com***

Made in the USA
Columbia, SC
28 February 2022